I Want to Trust, But Just Can't

Embracing God's Guidance Amidst Skepticism and Uncertainty

SABINA AUGUSTINA

Copyright © 2024 SABINA AUGUSTINA

All rights reserved. No part of this book may be reproduced or transmitted in any form or by any means, electronic or mechanical, including photocopying, recording, or by any information storage and retrieval system, without permission in writing from the publisher.

Disclaimer

This book is intended to provide spiritual guidance and encouragement for those navigating doubt and uncertainty in their faith journey. It is not a substitute for professional counseling or therapy. If you are struggling with severe anxiety, depression, or other mental health challenges, please seek help from a qualified healthcare provider.

While the author has made every effort to provide accurate and biblically sound information, the content of this book is based on personal experiences and interpretations of Scripture. It is not intended to be a definitive theological treatise or a comprehensive guide to overcoming doubt.

The reader is encouraged to use this book as a tool for reflection, prayer, and personal growth. Ultimately, the responsibility for cultivating trust in God rests with the individual, guided by the Holy Spirit and the wisdom of the Christian community.

DEDICATION

To those who wrestle with doubt, yet yearn for trust.

To those who feel lost, yet long to be found.

To those who question, yet seek to believe.

May this book be a light in your darkness, A guide on your journey, and a reminder that you are not alone.

May you find hope in God's unwavering love, Strength in His unfailing promises, and peace in His perfect plan.

With love and prayers,

Sabina Augustina

ACKNOWLEDGEMENT

First and foremost, I extend my deepest gratitude to God, the source of all wisdom and strength. Without His unwavering love and guidance, this book would not have been possible. His Word has been a lamp unto my feet and a light unto my path, illuminating the journey through doubt and uncertainty.

To my family, who have supported me throughout this process, thank you for your patience, understanding, and endless encouragement. Your love has been a constant reminder of God's faithfulness in my life.

To my church community, thank you for being a safe space where I can share my struggles and find solace in fellowship. Your prayers and support have carried me through moments of doubt and helped me rediscover the joy of trusting in God.

To my readers, I hope this book speaks to your hearts and provides guidance on your own faith journeys. May it remind you that you are not alone in your doubts and that God's love is always available, even in the midst of uncertainty.

Finally, to all those who have struggled with trust, may this book serve as a beacon of hope, reminding you that with God, all things are possible. May you find the courage to embrace His guidance and walk boldly in faith, even when the path ahead seems unclear.

TABLE OF CONTENTS

How to Use This Book 1
INTRODUCTION 3
Understanding Doubt as Part of Faith 7
    Acknowledging doubt without guilt 9
    Historical perspectives on doubt in
    Christianity 12
    The Role of Doubt in Spiritual Growth 15
Examining Personal Struggles with Trust 19
    Identifying Sources of Skepticism 21
    Impact of past experiences on trust 25
    Self-reflection exercises for understanding
    doubt 28
Seeking Divine Reassurance Through Scripture
.... 33
    Scriptural Promises About Trust 35
    Meditating on God's Faithfulness 38
    Applying Biblical Teachings to Present
    Struggles 42
The Power of Prayer in Overcoming Doubt 46
    Developing a consistent prayer life 48
    Examples of prayers for reassurance 52
    Listening for God's guidance in prayer 56
**Community Support: Strengthening Each
Other's Faith** 59

Finding Supportive Faith Groups.............. 62
Sharing Testimonies of Trust and Doubt..... 66
Encouraging Accountability Partnerships ... 69
Learning from Biblical Figures Who Faced Doubt.. **73**
Jacob Wrestling with God............................ 75
Abraham's journey of faith 77
Practical Steps for Building Faith.................. **86**
Daily devotionals and reflections 88
Incorporating worship into daily routine .. 119
Navigating Life Transitions with Faith **123**
Handling Loss and Grief with Faith 125
Trusting God's Plan during Career Changes
.... 127
Maintaining Faith Through Illness 130
Overcoming External Skepticism and Influences **134**
Understanding Emotional Triggers 137
Strengthening Internal Convictions 140
Living a Balanced Life **144**
Biblical foundations for hope 145
Personal stories of overcoming uncertainty
.... 148
Living out hope in daily actions 151
Moving Forward with Renewed Faith........... **154**

Setting Future Faith Goals......................... 155
Creating a Spiritual Growth Plan................ 158
Continuously Seeking God's Guidance...... 162
Conclusion.. 165

How to Use This Book

This book, "**I Want to Trust, But Just Can't: Embracing God's Guidance Amidst Skepticism and Uncertainty**," is your companion on a transformative journey towards deeper trust in God, even when doubts cloud your path. It's not a quick fix or a magic formula, but rather a gentle guide, inviting you to explore the complexities of faith with honesty, vulnerability, and a willingness to surrender to God's loving embrace.

Here are a few suggestions to make the most of this book:

- **Read prayerfully:** Before you begin each chapter, take a moment to invite the Holy Spirit to illuminate your heart and mind. Ask God to speak to you through these pages, to challenge your assumptions, and to deepen your trust in Him.

- **Reflect and engage:** At the end of each chapter, you'll find thought-provoking questions designed to spark personal reflection and application. Take time to ponder these questions, journal your thoughts, and engage in honest conversations with God about your struggles and hopes.

- **Embrace community:** Don't walk this journey alone. Share your insights and experiences with trusted friends, family members, or a faith community. Seek out mentors who can offer guidance and support. Remember, we are stronger together, and the collective wisdom of the body of Christ can be a powerful source of encouragement and strength.

- **Be patient and persistent:** Overcoming doubt and cultivating trust is a lifelong process. There will be setbacks and moments of discouragement. But don't give up. Keep seeking God's face, keep knocking on the door of His heart, and trust that He will faithfully lead you through the valleys of uncertainty and into the fullness of His love.

- **Practice what you learn:** Faith is not just about knowledge; it's about action. As you read this book, look for practical steps you can take to deepen your trust in God. This might involve spending more time in prayer, studying Scripture, serving others, or simply being more intentional about recognizing His presence in your daily life.

May this book be a source of comfort, encouragement, and spiritual growth as you navigate the complexities of faith. May it remind you that you are not alone in your struggles, that God is with you, and that He is able to do immeasurably more than all we ask or imagine, according to His power that is at work within us.

INTRODUCTION

Have you ever found yourself caught in the tension between wanting to fully trust God and feeling overwhelmed by troubling questions? It's a struggle that many of us face, often feeling as though we're walking a tightrope between faith and uncertainty. We long to surrender to God's will, yet nagging doubts creep in, whispering uncertainties that threaten to unravel our beliefs. It can be a lonely and isolating experience, leaving us feeling adrift in a sea of questions.

Perhaps you've questioned God's presence in the midst of suffering, wondering where He is when you need Him most. Maybe you've doubted His promises, fearing they are too good to be true. Or perhaps you've simply struggled to reconcile the complexities of life with the simplicity of your faith. These doubts, while often uncomfortable, are not signs of weakness or a lack of faith. They are, in fact, a natural part of the human experience, even within the context of a deep and abiding relationship with God.

Walking in the Footsteps of Faith

When we look at the lives of biblical figures, we see that questioning and grappling with faith is a timeless experience. Abraham, revered as the father of faith, questioned God's plan for his descendants, even after receiving a divine promise. Job, a man known for his righteousness, questioned God's justice in the face of immense suffering. And Jacob, wrestling with an angel throughout the night, wrestled with his own fears and uncertainties before receiving a blessing.

These stories remind us that even the most revered figures in Scripture dealt with uncertainty. They questioned, they doubted, and they struggled to reconcile their experiences with their faith. Yet, through their struggles, they emerged with a deeper understanding of God's character and a renewed commitment to trust in His plans. Their journeys serve as a beacon of hope for us, reminding us that doubt does not disqualify us from experiencing God's love and grace.

Embracing the Journey

Faith is not a static state; it's a dynamic journey filled with twists, turns, and unexpected detours. It's not about arriving at a destination where all doubts are erased and every question answered. Rather, it's about learning to walk hand-in-hand with God, even when the path ahead seems unclear. Doubt, in this context, can be a catalyst for growth, prompting us to seek deeper understanding and a more intimate connection with our Creator.

Just as a seed must break open to sprout and grow, our faith often flourishes in the very moments we wrestle with our questions. Doubt can lead us to explore Scripture more deeply, to engage in honest conversations with God, and to seek wisdom from trusted mentors and spiritual leaders. It can challenge us to examine our beliefs, refine our understanding, and ultimately emerge with a faith that is more resilient and authentic.

From Questions to Trust

This book is not about providing easy answers or dismissing your doubts. It's about inviting you to embrace the journey of faith, even when it feels messy and uncertain. It's about equipping you with tools and strategies to navigate the landscape of doubt, to find strength in God's Word, and to cultivate a deeper trust in His unwavering love.

In these pages, you will find practical steps for turning your struggles into pathways for trust. This isn't just about knowing; it's about doing—finding ways to actively engage with your faith even when doubts arise. We will explore biblical stories of doubt and faith, gleaning wisdom from those who have walked this path before us. We will delve into the power of prayer, the importance of community, and the transformative potential of surrendering our questions to God.

A Unique Approach

While many books address the topic of doubt, this one offers a unique perspective. It combines personal anecdotes with biblical insights, weaving together relatable stories with timeless truths. It invites you to journey alongside individuals who have wrestled with similar questions, finding solace and strength in their shared experiences. Moreover, it offers practical exercises and reflection questions to help you apply these principles to your own life.

This book is not a magic formula for eradicating doubt. It's a compass, pointing you towards the unwavering love and guidance of God. It's an invitation to embrace the journey of faith, to walk boldly into the unknown, trusting that God is with you every step of the way. Whether you're currently grappling with intense doubts or simply seeking to deepen your trust in God, this book will offer you hope, encouragement, and practical tools for navigating the complexities of faith.

It's time to move beyond the limitations of doubt and embrace the boundless possibilities of trust. Let's embark on this journey together, discovering the transformative power of faith in the midst of uncertainty.

Understanding Doubt as Part of Faith

Doubt is a natural and expected part of the Christian faith journey. It's the quiet whisper in the back of your mind, the nagging question that lingers despite your best efforts to push it away. You may wonder, "Does God really hear my prayers?" or "Is the Bible truly God's Word?" These doubts, while often uncomfortable, are not signs of weakness or a lack of faith. They are, in fact, a testament to the human condition – a condition marked by both a longing for the divine and a struggle to fully comprehend it.

In the Bible, we see numerous examples of individuals wrestling with doubt. Thomas, one of Jesus' disciples, famously refused to believe in the resurrection until he could see and touch Jesus' wounds. Even Jesus himself, in the Garden of Gethsemane, expressed a profound sense of anguish and uncertainty, asking God if there was another way to fulfill His will. These stories remind us that doubt is not a modern phenomenon; it's an age-old struggle that has been experienced by countless believers throughout history.

The Christian faith is not about blind acceptance or suppressing questions. It's about a dynamic relationship with God – one that involves both trust and inquiry. Doubt, when approached with humility and openness, can lead to a deeper understanding of God and a stronger faith.

It can prompt us to explore Scripture more deeply, to engage in honest conversations with God, and to seek wisdom from trusted mentors and spiritual leaders.

Rather than fearing doubt, we can learn to embrace it as a natural part of our spiritual growth. It can be a catalyst for transformation, prompting us to examine our beliefs, refine our understanding, and ultimately emerge with a faith that is more resilient and authentic. It's in the wrestling with our questions that we often find the greatest clarity and the most profound sense of connection with God.

Just as a muscle grows stronger through resistance training, our faith can be strengthened through the challenges of doubt. By facing our uncertainties head-on and seeking God's guidance, we can develop a deeper trust in His love and faithfulness. We can learn to lean on Him, even when we don't have all the answers, and to find peace in the midst of life's storms.

In the following chapters, we will explore the various facets of doubt, offering practical strategies for navigating its complexities and embracing its transformative potential. We will delve into the biblical narratives of those who wrestled with doubt, learning from their experiences and finding inspiration in their resilience. We will also examine the role of prayer, community, and spiritual practices in strengthening our faith and fostering a deeper trust in God.

Remember, doubt is not the enemy of faith; it's an invitation to a deeper relationship with the One who holds all the answers.

Acknowledging doubt without guilt

Doubt, an unwelcome guest in the quiet corners of our faith, often arrives draped in a cloak of guilt. We grapple not only with the questions themselves but with the shame of questioning. It feels as if our doubts betray a deficiency in our faith, a personal failure to fully embrace God's truth. But this self-condemnation, though common, is a heavy burden we need not bear.

The Christian faith is not a rigid edifice built on unwavering certainty. It is, rather, a dynamic relationship with God – a journey marked by both soaring moments of trust and quiet valleys of doubt. To experience doubt is not to forfeit your faith; it is to acknowledge the vastness of God and the limits of human understanding. It's a recognition that we are finite beings grappling with an infinite God, a God whose ways are higher than our ways, whose thoughts are higher than our thoughts.

The Bible, in its honesty and authenticity, does not shy away from portraying individuals wrestling with doubt. From Abraham's questioning of God's promises to Job's lament in the face of suffering, we witness a tapestry of human emotions woven into the fabric of faith. These stories remind us that doubt is not an anomaly but an integral part of the human experience, even within the context of deep devotion to God.

Jesus himself, fully human and fully divine, experienced moments of profound anguish and uncertainty. In the Garden of Gethsemane, He prayed, "*Father, if you are willing, take this cup from me; yet not my will, but yours be done.*" Here, we see Jesus grappling with the weight of His impending crucifixion, expressing a natural human desire to avoid suffering. Yet, He ultimately surrenders to God's will, demonstrating a profound trust even in the midst of doubt.

If Jesus, the Son of God, could experience doubt, then surely we, as imperfect beings, can extend ourselves the same grace. Our doubts do not diminish our faith; they simply reveal our humanity. They are a reminder that we are still on a journey, still growing in our understanding of God and His ways.

Embracing doubt without guilt requires a shift in perspective. Instead of viewing doubt as a sign of failure, we can reframe it as an opportunity for growth. When we acknowledge our doubts honestly and openly, we create space for deeper conversations with God. We can bring our questions to Him, trusting that He is big enough to handle our uncertainties and that He desires to lead us into a more profound understanding of His truth.

Furthermore, acknowledging doubt can foster a greater sense of connection within the Christian community. When we share our struggles openly, we create space for others to do the same. We discover that we are not alone in our questions, that many others are wrestling with similar uncertainties. This shared vulnerability can lead to deeper relationships, mutual encouragement, and a collective pursuit of truth.

Imagine a group of friends gathered around a campfire, sharing their deepest fears and questions about faith. In this safe space, doubts are not met with judgment but with empathy and understanding. Each person feels heard and valued, and together, they embark on a journey of discovery, seeking God's wisdom and guidance. This is the power of acknowledging doubt without guilt – it opens the door to authentic connection and shared spiritual growth.

It's important to remember that doubt is not synonymous with disbelief. You can doubt specific aspects of your faith while still holding onto a core belief in God's love and faithfulness. Just as a child may question their parents' decisions while still trusting in their love, we can question God's ways while still clinging to the foundational truth of His goodness.

In fact, doubt can even serve as a catalyst for strengthening our faith. When we wrestle with our questions and seek answers in God's Word and through prayer, we often emerge with a deeper conviction and a more mature faith. The process of questioning can lead us to a more nuanced understanding of God's character and His plan for our lives.

So, let us shed the heavy cloak of guilt and embrace our doubts with courage and honesty. Let us bring our questions to God, trusting that He will meet us in our uncertainties and lead us into a deeper relationship with Him. Let us share our struggles with others, finding strength and encouragement in the shared journey of faith. And let us remember that doubt, when approached with humility and openness, can be a powerful tool for spiritual growth and transformation.

In the words of the apostle Paul, *"For now we see only a reflection as in a mirror; then we shall see face to face. Now I know in part; then I shall know fully, even as I am fully known."* Our faith is a journey of discovery, a gradual unfolding of God's truth in our lives. Doubt is not an obstacle to be overcome but a natural part of that journey, a reminder that we are still growing, still learning, still seeking to know God more fully.

Historical perspectives on doubt in Christianity

The echoes of doubt reverberate through the corridors of Christian history, whispering a truth often overlooked: questioning and wrestling with faith is not a modern anomaly but an enduring thread woven into the very fabric of our spiritual heritage. From the earliest pages of Scripture to the pulpits of today, the voices of those who have grappled with uncertainty remind us that doubt is not an aberration but an integral part of the human experience with God.

In the Bible, we encounter a multitude of individuals who, despite their deep devotion to God, expressed moments of profound doubt. Thomas, known as "Doubting Thomas," famously refused to believe in Jesus' resurrection until he could see and touch the wounds in His hands and side. His skepticism, though ultimately overcome by a personal encounter with the risen Christ, serves as a powerful reminder that even those closest to Jesus experienced moments of questioning. Peter, another disciple, denied knowing Jesus three times in the hours leading up to the crucifixion, his fear overshadowing his faith. Yet, he was later restored and became a pillar of the early church.

The Old Testament is also rife with examples of doubt. Moses, chosen by God to lead the Israelites out of Egypt, questioned his own abilities and the feasibility of God's plan. The Israelites themselves, despite witnessing countless miracles, frequently doubted God's provision and guidance, yearning for the comforts of their former lives. These stories, woven into the tapestry of Scripture, affirm that doubt has always been part of the human experience with God.

Throughout church history, theologians and leaders have wrestled with doubt, their struggles often shaping the very course of Christian thought. Augustine of Hippo, one of the most influential figures in Western Christianity, spent years grappling with questions about faith and reason before ultimately embracing Christianity. Martin Luther, the catalyst for the Protestant Reformation, experienced deep spiritual crises and doubts about his own salvation.

Their writings and teachings reflect a profound honesty about the challenges of faith, offering solace and guidance to countless believers who have followed in their footsteps.

The Reformation itself was a period of intense questioning and debate, as Christians grappled with issues of authority, interpretation, and the nature of salvation. This era of upheaval and transformation demonstrates that doubt can be a powerful force for change, leading to new insights and a deeper understanding of God's truth.

In more recent times, figures like C.S. Lewis and Mother Teresa have openly shared their own struggles with doubt, reminding us that even those revered for their faith can experience moments of uncertainty. Their honesty and vulnerability resonate with countless believers today, offering comfort and encouragement in the face of our own questions.

The growing acceptance of doubt within many faith communities is reflected in the increasing number of books, sermons, and conferences addressing this topic. Contemporary theologians and pastors are engaging in open and honest conversations about the complexities of faith, acknowledging that doubt is not a sign of weakness but a natural part of the spiritual journey.

Furthermore, the historical response to doubt has given rise to a variety of spiritual practices aimed at strengthening faith and navigating uncertainty. The practice of lament, for example, rooted in the Psalms and other biblical texts, provides a space for expressing sorrow, anger, and even doubt towards God. The tradition of questioning God, exemplified by figures like Job and Habakkuk, invites us to bring our honest inquiries before Him, trusting that He can handle our doubts and lead us into a deeper understanding of His ways.

These practices, along with others like contemplative prayer and spiritual direction, offer pathways for engaging with doubt in a healthy and constructive way. They remind us that doubt need not be a source of isolation or shame but can, in fact, be a catalyst for spiritual growth and a deeper connection with God.

The Role of Doubt in Spiritual Growth

Doubt, often perceived as a stumbling block on the path of faith, can paradoxically serve as a catalyst for profound spiritual growth. Like a sculptor's chisel that reveals the beauty hidden within a block of marble, doubt can chip away at our preconceived notions and reveal a deeper, more authentic faith.

When questions arise, when uncertainties cloud our understanding, we are compelled to seek answers. This pursuit of clarity often leads to a more profound exploration of Scripture, theological teachings, and the lived experiences of others. It's in the wrestling with our doubts that we delve deeper into the heart of our faith, seeking not just answers but a deeper connection with the God who invites us to question and explore.

The impulse to resolve doubt can also inspire a renewal in our spiritual practices. We may find ourselves drawn to prayer with a newfound intensity, seeking solace and guidance in the midst of our uncertainties. We may turn to the wisdom of spiritual mentors or engage in thoughtful conversations with fellow believers, seeking to understand how others have navigated similar challenges. In this way, doubt can act as a springboard for a more vibrant and intentional faith life.

Furthermore, doubt encourages us to examine and test the foundations of our beliefs. It forces us to confront any inconsistencies or misconceptions we may have about God, His character, and His plans for our lives. This process of self-examination can be uncomfortable, but it ultimately leads to a stronger, more resilient faith built on a solid foundation of understanding and personal conviction.

As we wrestle with our doubts, we also develop a greater empathy for others who are on a similar journey. We recognize that we are not alone in our struggles, that many others are grappling with questions and uncertainties. This shared experience can foster a deeper sense of connection within the Christian community, creating space for open and honest conversations about faith. It can also empower us to offer support and encouragement to those who are navigating their own doubts, drawing on our own experiences to provide guidance and hope.

The journey through doubt, though often challenging, can ultimately lead to a richer and more dynamic spiritual life. When we emerge on the other side of our questions, we often find that our faith has been refined and strengthened. We have a deeper appreciation for the complexities of God's truth, a greater sense of awe for His mysterious ways, and a more profound trust in His unwavering love.

Moreover, overcoming doubt can yield powerful personal testimonies of God's faithfulness. When we share our stories of wrestling with questions and ultimately finding peace in God's presence, we offer hope to others who are on a similar path. Our experiences become a beacon of light, illuminating the way for those who are still navigating the darkness of doubt.

Recognizing how past doubts have led to spiritual growth can also inspire confidence in God's future plans for our lives. We can trust that even when new questions arise, He will be there to guide us, to provide wisdom and strength, and to lead us into a deeper relationship with Him. We can embrace the unknown with a sense of anticipation, knowing that God is working all things together for our good, even in the midst of uncertainty.

In essence, doubt is not a barrier to faith but a crucial element for spiritual growth. It's an invitation to explore, to question, and to seek a deeper understanding of God and His ways. It's a reminder that faith is not about blind acceptance but about an ongoing relationship with the One who invites us to come to Him with all our questions and concerns.

As you continue your journey of faith, remember that doubt is not something to be feared or suppressed. It's an opportunity for growth, for deeper connection with God and with others, and for a more authentic and vibrant faith life. Embrace your doubts, wrestle with your questions, and trust that God will meet you in the midst of your uncertainties, leading you into a deeper relationship with Him.

Examining Personal Struggles with Trust

"The heart is deceitful above all things, and desperately sick; who can understand it?" (Jeremiah 17:9, ESV)

This ancient wisdom, penned by the prophet Jeremiah, speaks to a fundamental truth about the human condition: our hearts, the seat of our emotions and desires, are prone to deception and self-protection. When it comes to trusting God, this inherent fallibility can manifest in a myriad of ways, shaping our perceptions, influencing our decisions, and ultimately hindering our ability to fully surrender to His will.

To embark on a journey of trust, we must first acknowledge the complexities of our own hearts. We must recognize that our past experiences, both positive and negative, have left an indelible mark on our souls, shaping our beliefs about God, ourselves, and the world around us. Unmet expectations, broken promises, and painful losses can create deep wounds that make it difficult to trust, even in the face of God's unwavering love.

Perhaps you grew up in an environment where trust was a fragile commodity, where promises were easily broken and vulnerability was met with betrayal. These early experiences may have instilled in you a deep-seated skepticism, making it difficult to believe in God's promises or to rely on His provision. Or perhaps you have experienced personal setbacks or disappointments that have shaken your faith, leaving you questioning God's goodness and His plans for your life.

These past experiences, though often painful, are not meant to be ignored or suppressed. They are part of your story, and they have shaped you into the person you are today. By acknowledging their impact on your ability to trust, you take an important step towards healing and wholeness. You create space for God to enter into those wounded places and bring His comfort and restoration.

In addition to past experiences, there may be specific triggers that ignite your doubts and uncertainties. These triggers can be situations, people, or even thoughts that evoke a sense of fear, anxiety, or vulnerability. Perhaps you feel a surge of doubt when faced with a difficult decision, unsure of which path to choose. Or maybe you experience a sense of skepticism when encountering those who express unwavering certainty about their faith.

Identifying these triggers is a crucial step in understanding your personal struggles with trust. It allows you to anticipate potential challenges and to develop strategies for navigating them with God's help. By recognizing the situations or thoughts that tend to spark your doubts, you can proactively seek God's guidance and strength, arming yourself against the onslaught of uncertainty.

As you examine your personal struggles with trust, remember that you are not alone. Countless believers throughout history have wrestled with similar questions and uncertainties. The Psalms, for example, are filled with expressions of doubt, fear, and even anger towards God. These raw and honest prayers remind us that it's okay to bring our full range of emotions before God, trusting that He can handle our doubts and lead us into a deeper relationship with Him.

The journey towards trust is not a linear one. There will be setbacks and moments of discouragement. But with each step, with each honest conversation with God, and with each act of surrender to His will, you will find your faith growing stronger and your trust deepening. It's in the wrestling with our doubts that we discover the true strength and resilience of our faith.

Identifying Sources of Skepticism

In our quest to understand and overcome the barriers that hinder trust in God, it's essential to shine a light on the often-subtle influences that shape our perceptions and fuel our skepticism. Like hidden currents beneath the surface of a calm sea, these sources of doubt can subtly erode our faith, leaving us feeling adrift and uncertain.

Let's begin by examining the impact of external influences. We live in a world saturated with messages that challenge or even mock religious beliefs. From the relentless pursuit of material success to the glorification of self-reliance, societal expectations can subtly undermine our trust in God's provision and guidance. Media portrayals of religious hypocrisy and scandals can further fuel our doubts, painting a picture of faith as something outdated or even harmful. Even well-meaning friends or colleagues may express skepticism about religious beliefs, their questions and doubts inadvertently sowing seeds of uncertainty in our own minds.

These external influences, though often subtle, can exert a powerful pull on our hearts and minds. We may find ourselves questioning the validity of our faith, wondering if it's truly relevant in a world that seems increasingly secular and skeptical. We may feel a sense of isolation or inadequacy, as if our beliefs are out of step with the prevailing cultural narrative. It's important to recognize that these feelings are not uncommon. Many believers throughout history have wrestled with the tension between their faith and the prevailing cultural currents of their time.

However, it's equally important to remember that we are not passive recipients of external influences. We have the power to discern which voices are healthy and life-giving, and which are detrimental to our spiritual well-being. We can choose to surround ourselves with people who uplift and encourage us in our faith, and we can actively seek out resources that strengthen our understanding of God's truth. By being intentional about the influences we allow into our lives, we can create a space where our faith can flourish, even in the midst of a skeptical world.

Personal relationships can also play a significant role in shaping our trust in God. When those we love and respect express doubt or cynicism about faith, it can be deeply unsettling. We may question our own beliefs, wondering if we've been misled or if we're simply naive for believing in something that others find so easily dismissed. Conversely, healthy and supportive relationships can be a source of immense strength and encouragement. Mentors who have walked the path of faith before us can offer wisdom and guidance, helping us navigate our own doubts and uncertainties. Friends who share our beliefs can provide a safe space for honest conversations about faith, creating a sense of belonging and mutual support.

It's important to recognize that not all relationships are created equal. Some may be toxic, undermining our faith and leaving us feeling isolated and discouraged. In such cases, it may be necessary to set boundaries or even distance ourselves from those who consistently challenge or belittle our beliefs. We are called to love others, but we are not obligated to subject ourselves to constant negativity or criticism. By prioritizing healthy relationships and seeking out mentors who can guide us on our faith journey, we create a support system that fosters trust and encourages spiritual growth.

Another common source of skepticism is the tendency to compare our faith journey to that of others. We may look at those who seem to have unwavering faith, who never seem to struggle with doubt or uncertainty, and wonder what's wrong with us. We may feel inadequate or even ashamed of our own questions and struggles, believing that we're somehow failing in our faith.

However, this comparison trap is a dangerous one. It obscures the reality that faith is a deeply personal journey, one that unfolds in unique ways for each individual. Some may experience a sudden and dramatic conversion, while others may come to faith gradually, through a series of small steps and subtle shifts in perspective. Some may rarely experience doubt, while others may wrestle with questions throughout their lives.

The key is to focus on your own journey, not on the perceived progress of others. Celebrate your own growth, no matter how small or incremental it may seem. Recognize that doubt is a natural part of the faith journey, and that it can even be a catalyst for deeper understanding and a more authentic relationship with God. By embracing your own unique path and resisting the urge to compare yourself to others, you create space for God to work in your life in His own way and in His own time.

Finally, it's important to acknowledge the impact of life's crises on our faith. When we experience loss, trauma, or profound disappointment, it can shake the very foundations of our beliefs. We may question God's goodness, His sovereignty, or even His existence. These moments of crisis can be incredibly disorienting, leaving us feeling lost and alone in a world that suddenly seems devoid of meaning.

It's important to recognize that these feelings are normal and natural. When we're in the midst of a crisis, it's easy to lose sight of God's presence and His promises. Our pain and confusion can cloud our vision, making it difficult to see beyond the immediate circumstances. However, it's precisely in these moments of darkness that we need to cling to our faith most tightly. We need to remind ourselves that God is still with us, even when we can't feel His presence. We need to trust that He is working all things together for our good, even when we can't see how.

Impact of past experiences on trust

Our past experiences, like the layers of sediment that form the foundation of a riverbed, shape the contours of our faith journey. The joys and sorrows, triumphs and setbacks, blessings and betrayals we've encountered throughout our lives leave an indelible mark on our hearts, influencing our ability to trust in God.

Unresolved past traumas, in particular, can cast long shadows of doubt and skepticism. When we've experienced deep hurt or betrayal, whether at the hands of others or through circumstances beyond our control, it can be difficult to reconcile those experiences with a belief in a loving and benevolent God. We may question His goodness, His sovereignty, or even His very existence.

The wounds of the past, if left unattended, can fester and grow, creating barriers to experiencing God's love and grace. Fear, anxiety, and bitterness can take root in our hearts, making it difficult to fully surrender to His will.

We may find ourselves hesitant to trust, even in the face of His promises, our past experiences whispering warnings of potential pain and disappointment.

Healing from these past traumas is a crucial step in rebuilding trust in God. It's a process that requires courage, vulnerability, and a willingness to confront the pain that has been buried deep within. It may involve seeking professional counseling, engaging in prayer and meditation, or simply spending time in quiet reflection, allowing God to speak into the wounded places of your heart.

Remember, healing is not an overnight process. It takes time, patience, and a deep reliance on God's grace. But as you allow Him to enter into those dark corners of your past, you will find that He brings light, healing, and a renewed sense of hope. You will discover that His love is greater than any pain you've experienced, and that He is able to redeem even the most broken parts of your story.

While past traumas can undoubtedly create challenges to trust, it's equally important to acknowledge the positive experiences that have bolstered your faith. Remember those moments when you felt God's presence most tangibly, when His love and faithfulness were undeniable. Recall the times when He answered your prayers, provided for your needs, or brought comfort in the midst of sorrow.

These memories are precious treasures, reminders of God's goodness and His unwavering commitment to you.

Take time to reflect on these experiences, allowing them to fill your heart with gratitude and appreciation. Consider creating a "faith timeline," recording the specific instances when God has intervened in your life or shown you His love in a tangible way. This visual reminder can be a source of encouragement during times of doubt, reminding you that God has been faithful in the past and that He will continue to be faithful in the future.

In addition to personal experiences, it's important to consider how your family background and cultural influences have shaped your ability to trust in God. The messages you received about faith as a child, the religious practices you observed in your family, and the cultural narratives surrounding religion can all play a role in your current beliefs and attitudes.

If you grew up in a loving and supportive Christian home, you may have developed a strong foundation of trust in God from an early age. However, if your family background was marked by religious conflict, hypocrisy, or legalism, you may struggle to reconcile those experiences with a genuine faith in a loving God. Similarly, if you come from a culture that views religion with skepticism or hostility, you may find it challenging to fully embrace your faith in the face of societal pressures.

Recognizing these influences is an important step in understanding your own faith journey. It allows you to identify any harmful beliefs or attitudes that you may have internalized and to begin the process of reshaping your faith narrative. It's also an opportunity to appreciate the positive aspects of your background, recognizing the ways in which your family and culture have contributed to your spiritual development.

Finally, it's important to acknowledge that the journey of faith is not always a smooth one. There will be times when your trust in God wavers, when doubts and uncertainties cloud your vision. These cycles of doubt and faith are a normal part of the human experience, and they can even be opportunities for growth and transformation.

When you find yourself caught in a cycle of doubt, it's important to be patient with yourself. Don't beat yourself up for your questions or your struggles. Instead, recognize that these are natural responses to the complexities of life and the vastness of God. Seek out trusted mentors or spiritual leaders who can offer guidance and support. Engage in practices that nourish your soul and draw you closer to God, such as prayer, meditation, and Scripture reading.

Self-reflection exercises for understanding doubt

In the quiet moments of introspection, we find the space to unravel the knots of doubt that tangle our faith. Through intentional self-reflection, we can illuminate the hidden corners of our hearts, bringing our questions and uncertainties into the light of God's truth.

"Search me, O God, and know my heart! Try me and know my thoughts! And see if there be any grievous way in me, and lead me in the way everlasting!" (Psalm 139:23-24, ESV). This timeless plea, penned by King David, invites us to engage in a journey of self-discovery, to lay bare our deepest fears and doubts before the One who knows us intimately.

One powerful tool for this journey is journaling. By putting pen to paper, we create a sacred space for honest dialogue with ourselves and with God. Consider these journaling prompts as you begin to explore your own struggles with trust:

- What specific situations or experiences trigger feelings of doubt in my faith?
- Are there any recurring patterns or themes in my doubts?
- What are the underlying fears or anxieties that fuel my skepticism?
- How do my past experiences, both positive and negative, influence my ability to trust in God?
- What are the specific promises or aspects of my faith that I find most difficult to believe?

As you write, allow your thoughts and emotions to flow freely. Don't censor yourself or try to present a polished version of your faith. Instead, be honest and vulnerable, pouring out your heart to God as you would to a trusted friend. Remember, He already knows the depths of your heart; He longs for you to share them with Him openly and without fear.

Another powerful practice for confronting doubt is prayer. Prayer is not simply a recitation of requests or a means of expressing gratitude; it's a conversation with God, an opportunity to share our deepest longings, fears, and questions. When we pray through our doubts, we invite God into the messy and uncertain places of our hearts. We acknowledge that we don't have all the answers, and we seek His guidance and wisdom.

Consider these prayer reflections as you navigate your own doubts:

- "Lord, I want to trust you, but I'm struggling with doubt. Please help me to understand the source of my skepticism and to find peace in your presence."
- "God, I'm afraid to be honest about my doubts, but I know you see my heart. Please give me the courage to bring my questions to you and to trust in your love and faithfulness."
- "Father, I'm feeling lost and uncertain. Please guide me through this season of doubt and help me to rediscover the joy of trusting in you."

As you pray, remember that God is not intimidated by your questions or your doubts. He welcomes your honesty and vulnerability, and He longs to meet you in the midst of your struggles. Allow your prayers to be a conversation, not a monologue. Listen for His still, small voice, and trust that He will lead you into a deeper understanding of His truth.

If you're part of a faith community, consider engaging in group discussions about trust and doubt. Sharing your experiences with others can be incredibly liberating, reminding you that you're not alone in your struggles. It can also create opportunities for mutual encouragement and support, as you learn from the wisdom and experiences of others.

Here are a few prompts to facilitate group discussions:

- Share a time when you experienced doubt in your faith. What triggered those doubts, and how did you navigate them?
- What are some of the common sources of skepticism within our culture, and how can we respond to them with grace and truth?
- How can we support one another when we're going through seasons of doubt?
- What are some practical steps we can take to strengthen our trust in God, even when we're facing challenges or uncertainties?

These discussions can be a powerful source of connection and growth, fostering a sense of belonging and mutual support within the community. They can also provide opportunities to learn from the diverse perspectives and experiences of others, enriching your own understanding of faith and doubt.

Finally, consider incorporating reflective meditation into your spiritual practice. Choose a passage of Scripture that speaks to the theme of trust, such as Psalm 23 or Proverbs 3:5-6. Read the passage slowly and prayerfully, allowing the words to sink deep into your heart. As you meditate on these truths, invite God to speak to you through His Word, offering reassurance and comfort in the midst of your doubts.

These self-reflection exercises, when practiced consistently and with an open heart, can lead to a profound transformation in your faith journey. They can help you to identify the root causes of your doubts, to develop strategies for navigating uncertainty, and to cultivate a deeper trust in God's love and faithfulness. Remember, doubt is not the enemy of faith; it's an invitation to a more intimate relationship with the One who holds all the answers. Embrace the journey of self-discovery, and allow God to lead you into a deeper understanding of His truth.

Seeking Divine Reassurance Through Scripture

"Your word is a lamp to my feet and a light to my path." (Psalm 119:105, ESV)

In the midst of doubt and uncertainty, when the path ahead seems shrouded in darkness, the Bible shines as a beacon of hope, offering guidance, comfort, and reassurance. Its pages are filled with stories of individuals who wrestled with their own questions and fears, yet ultimately found solace and strength in God's unwavering love and faithfulness. As we immerse ourselves in the Scriptures, we encounter a God who understands our struggles, who meets us in our moments of doubt, and who gently leads us back to a place of trust.

The Bible is not simply a collection of ancient texts; it's a living and active word, breathing life into our weary souls and illuminating the path towards a deeper relationship with God. It's a source of timeless wisdom, offering insights into the human condition, the nature of God, and the complexities of faith. As we read and meditate on its pages, we encounter a God who is both transcendent and immanent, both beyond our comprehension and intimately involved in our lives.

In the stories of biblical figures, we find echoes of our own doubts and fears. We see Abraham wrestling with the seemingly impossible promise of a son in his old age, Moses questioning his ability to lead the Israelites out of Egypt, and David pouring out his heart to God in moments of despair and confusion. These stories remind us that we are not alone in our struggles, that even the most faithful individuals in Scripture experienced moments of doubt and uncertainty.

But the Bible also offers countless examples of God's faithfulness, His unwavering love, and His power to transform even the most difficult circumstances. We see Him parting the Red Sea, providing manna in the wilderness, and raising Jesus from the dead. These stories remind us that God is not limited by our doubts or our fears. He is able to do immeasurably more than all we ask or imagine, and He invites us to trust in His promises, even when they seem impossible.

As we seek scriptural reassurance in times of doubt, we can turn to specific passages that speak directly to our struggles. The Psalms, for example, offer a rich tapestry of human emotions, from lament and despair to praise and thanksgiving. In these poetic expressions of faith, we find comfort in knowing that others have walked this path before us, and that God has heard and answered their cries.

The Gospels, too, offer a profound source of hope and encouragement. In the life and teachings of Jesus, we see a God who is compassionate, merciful, and full of grace. We witness His power to heal the sick, forgive the sinner, and restore the broken-hearted. His words, recorded in the Gospels, offer timeless wisdom and guidance for navigating the complexities of life and faith.

Beyond specific passages, the overarching narrative of the Bible itself is a testament to God's faithfulness. From the creation of the world to the promise of a new heaven and a new earth, we see a God who is actively working to redeem and restore all things. This grand story reminds us that our doubts and struggles are not the final word. God is still on the throne, and He is still writing our story, even in the midst of uncertainty.

As you engage with Scripture, allow it to speak to your heart and mind. Read it prayerfully, asking God to reveal His truth to you. Meditate on its words, allowing them to sink deep into your soul. And most importantly, trust that God will meet you in the pages of His Word, offering comfort, guidance, and a renewed sense of hope.

Scriptural Promises About Trust

When the waves of doubt crash against the shores of our faith, it's easy to feel overwhelmed and alone. The questions swirl, the uncertainties multiply, and we find ourselves longing for a firm foundation on which to stand. In these moments of vulnerability, we can turn to the timeless promises of Scripture, anchors for our souls in the midst of life's storms.

"Fear not, for I am with you; be not dismayed, for I am your God; I will strengthen you, I will help you, I will uphold you with my righteous right hand." **(Isaiah 41:10, ESV).** This powerful declaration from the prophet Isaiah speaks to the very heart of our longing for reassurance. It reminds us that even in the darkest valleys of doubt, we are not alone. God is with us, His presence a constant source of strength and comfort. He promises to strengthen us when we are weak, to help us when we are helpless, and to uphold us with His righteous right hand.

This promise is not an empty platitude; it's a lifeline for those who are struggling to trust. It invites us to lean into God's presence, to find refuge in His embrace, and to draw strength from His unwavering love. When doubts assail us, we can whisper this verse to ourselves, reminding ourselves that God is with us, even when we can't feel His presence. We can trust that He is working behind the scenes, orchestrating events for our good, even when we can't see the bigger picture.

In the New Testament, we encounter another powerful promise that speaks to our need for peace in the midst of turmoil. *"And the peace of God, which surpasses all understanding, will guard your hearts and your minds in Christ Jesus."* **(Philippians 4:7, ESV).** This peace is not the absence of conflict or struggle; it's a deep-seated tranquillity that transcends our circumstances. It's a sense of calm and assurance that comes from knowing that we are held in the loving hands of God.

When doubts and anxieties threaten to overwhelm us, we can cling to this promise of peace. We can surrender our worries to God, trusting that He will guard our hearts and minds, protecting us from the onslaught of negativity and fear. This peace is not something we can manufacture on our own; it's a gift from God, freely given to those who seek Him with a sincere heart.

As we look to the future, we may find ourselves grappling with doubts about God's plans for our lives. We may wonder if we're on the right path, if we're making the right choices, or if we'll ever achieve our dreams. In these moments of uncertainty, we can find solace in the words of Jeremiah 29:11: ***"For I know the plans I have for you, declares the Lord, plans for welfare and not for evil, to give you a future and a hope."***

This verse reminds us that God has a purpose for our lives, a plan that is good and filled with hope. Even when we can't see the road ahead, we can trust that He is leading us towards a future that is far greater than anything we could imagine. This knowledge can anchor us in times of doubt, reminding us that our lives are not random or meaningless. We are part of a larger story, a divine narrative that is unfolding according to God's perfect will.

Finally, we can find encouragement in the apostle Paul's words in 2 Corinthians 12:9: ***"But he said to me, 'My grace is sufficient for you, for my power is made perfect in weakness.' Therefore I will boast all the more gladly of my weaknesses, so that the power of Christ may rest***

upon me." This verse speaks to the transformative power of vulnerability. It reminds us that our weaknesses and limitations are not obstacles to God's work in our lives; they are, in fact, opportunities for His power to be displayed.

When we acknowledge our doubts and uncertainties, we open ourselves to God's grace and strength. We recognize that we are not self-sufficient, but that we are utterly dependent on Him. In our weakness, His power is made perfect. This realization can be incredibly liberating, freeing us from the burden of trying to have all the answers or to control every aspect of our lives.

These scriptural promises, and countless others like them, offer a wellspring of hope and encouragement for those who are struggling to trust. They remind us that God is faithful, even when we are faithless. They assure us that His love is steadfast, His plans are good, and His presence is constant. As we meditate on these promises, allowing them to take root in our hearts, we will find that our trust in God deepens, our doubts begin to fade, and our faith becomes a beacon of light in a world shrouded in darkness.

Meditating on God's Faithfulness

When doubts cast a shadow over our faith, it's easy to forget the countless ways God has proven His faithfulness throughout history and in our own lives. But like a lighthouse piercing through the fog, meditation on His past actions can illuminate our path, reminding us of His unwavering love and steadfast commitment.

The Old Testament unfolds a breath-taking panorama of God's miraculous interventions, each a testament to His unwavering faithfulness. The parting of the Red Sea, a dramatic display of divine power, allowed the Israelites to escape their Egyptian oppressors and embark on a journey towards freedom. The provision of manna in the wilderness, a daily reminder of God's provision, sustained them through their forty-year sojourn. These extraordinary events, etched into the annals of history, serve as a powerful reminder that God is not bound by the limitations of human understanding. He is able to do the impossible, to defy the laws of nature, and to fulfil His promises, even when they seem unattainable.

As we reflect on these stories, we are invited to see God's consistent actions throughout history as a testament to His reliability. We can trust that the God who parted the Red Sea is the same God who walks beside us today, ready to intervene on our behalf and guide us through the challenges we face. We can draw strength from the knowledge that He who provided manna in the wilderness is still our provider, capable of meeting our needs in ways we may not even anticipate.

But meditation on God's faithfulness is not limited to the grand narratives of the Bible. It also involves reflecting on our own personal experiences of His love and grace. Take a moment to recall those times when you felt God's presence most tangibly, when He answered your prayers, provided for your needs, or brought comfort in the midst of sorrow. These personal testimonies are a powerful reminder of God's ongoing work in our lives, evidence that He is not a distant deity but a loving Father who is intimately involved in our every step.

Perhaps you can remember a time when you faced a seemingly insurmountable obstacle, and God miraculously opened a door that you never thought possible. Or maybe you can recall a season of deep grief or loss, when God's comfort surrounded you like a warm embrace. These personal encounters with God, however small or seemingly insignificant, are woven into the fabric of your faith journey, creating a tapestry of His faithfulness that can sustain you in times of doubt.

Praying with Scripture is another powerful way to meditate on God's faithfulness. The Psalms, in particular, offer a rich source of prayers and meditations that express trust in God, even in the midst of trials and tribulations. **"The Lord is my shepherd; I shall not want." (Psalm 23:1, ESV)** This familiar verse, a declaration of complete dependence on God, reminds us that He is our provider, our protector, and our guide. We can trust that He will lead us beside still waters, restore our souls, and prepare a table for us in the presence of our enemies.

In addition to prayer and Scripture reading, contemplative practices can also be a valuable tool for meditating on God's faithfulness. In the silence and solitude of contemplation, we create space for God to speak to our hearts. We quiet the noise of the world and listen for His still, small voice, trusting that He will meet us in the stillness and reveal His truth to us.

Jesus himself often withdrew to solitary places to pray and commune with His Father. In the wilderness, He faced temptation and wrestled with His own humanity, yet He emerged with a renewed sense of purpose and a deeper reliance on God's strength. His example reminds us that solitude is not isolation; it's an opportunity to draw near to God and to receive His guidance and renewal.

As you engage in contemplative practices, be patient with yourself. It may take time to quiet your mind and to truly listen for God's voice. But as you persevere, you will find that these moments of stillness can yield profound insights into your faith journey. You may discover new depths of God's love, new facets of His character, and a renewed sense of trust in His faithfulness.

Meditating on God's faithfulness is not a one-time event; it's an ongoing practice that can sustain us through every season of life. By reflecting on His past actions, recalling our own experiences of His grace, praying with Scripture, and engaging in contemplative practices, we can cultivate a deep and abiding trust in God, even in the midst of skepticism and uncertainty.

Applying Biblical Teachings to Present Struggles

In times of doubt and uncertainty, the Bible serves as a compass, pointing us toward the unwavering truth of God's love and faithfulness. Its pages contain countless stories and teachings that resonate with our struggles, offering wisdom, comfort, and guidance for navigating the complexities of faith.

To apply these biblical teachings to our present struggles, we must first identify the specific areas where our trust is wavering. What questions are lingering in your mind? What fears are holding you back from fully surrendering to God's will? Are there specific situations or relationships that trigger feelings of doubt and skepticism?

Take some time to reflect on these questions, journaling your thoughts and feelings. Be honest with yourself about the challenges you're facing, and don't be afraid to express your doubts and uncertainties to God. He already knows the depths of your heart, and He longs for you to come to Him with your questions and concerns.

Once you've identified your areas of struggle, it's time to turn to Scripture for guidance and reassurance. The Bible is filled with verses that speak directly to the challenges we face, offering wisdom and comfort for every season of life.

If you're struggling with fear or anxiety, you might find solace in Isaiah 41:10: ***"Fear not, for I am with you; be*** *not dismayed, for I am your God; I will strengthen you, I will help you, I will uphold you with my righteous right hand."* This verse reminds us that God is always with us, even in the midst of our darkest fears. He promises to strengthen us, to help us, and to uphold us with His righteous right hand.

If you're feeling overwhelmed by life's challenges, you might turn to Matthew 11:28-30: *"Come to me, all who labour and are heavy laden, and I will give you rest. Take my yoke upon you, and learn from me, for I am gentle and lowly in heart, and you will find rest for your souls. For my yoke is easy, and my burden is light."* In these words, Jesus offers an invitation to find rest in Him, to exchange our heavy burdens for His light and easy yoke.

If you're struggling with feelings of inadequacy or unworthiness, you might find comfort in Romans 8:38-39: *"For I am sure that neither death nor life, nor angels nor rulers, nor things present nor things to come, nor powers, nor height nor depth, nor anything else in all creation, will be able to separate us from the love of God in Christ Jesus our Lord."* This powerful passage reminds us that nothing can separate us from God's love, not even our own failings or shortcomings.

As you search the Scriptures, look for verses that speak directly to your specific struggles. Use a concordance or Bible app to search for key words or themes that resonate with your current challenges. Pay attention to the context of the verses you find, seeking to understand their original meaning and how they apply to your life today.

But don't stop at simply reading and reflecting on Scripture. Take the next step and put its teachings into practice. If you're struggling to trust God's provision, for example, consider giving generously to others, even when you're feeling financially stretched. If you're doubting God's love for you, make a conscious effort to extend love and compassion to those around you.

These acts of obedience, even when they feel difficult or counterintuitive, can be powerful expressions of trust. They demonstrate that you're willing to step out in faith, even when you don't have all the answers. They also create opportunities for God to show Himself faithful, to provide for your needs, and to pour out His love in unexpected ways.

In addition to practical obedience, seeking accountability can also be a helpful tool for reinforcing trust in God. Share your struggles with a trusted friend, mentor, or pastor. Ask them to pray for you, to encourage you, and to hold you accountable for living out your faith. Joining a small group or Bible study can also provide a supportive community where you can share your doubts and questions, learn from others, and grow in your faith together.

Remember, the Christian life is not meant to be lived in isolation. We need the support and encouragement of others to help us navigate the challenges of faith. By surrounding ourselves with people who love God and who are committed to following Him, we create a network of support that can sustain us in times of doubt and uncertainty.

As you apply biblical teachings to your present struggles, remember that faith is a journey, not a destination. There will be ups and downs, moments of clarity and moments of confusion. But through it all, God is with you, offering His guidance, His comfort, and His unwavering love. By seeking His wisdom in Scripture, putting His teachings into practice, and surrounding yourself with a supportive community, you can navigate the complexities of faith with confidence, knowing that He is leading you towards a future filled with hope and purpose.

So, let us open our Bibles with expectant hearts, eager to discover the treasures of wisdom and truth that lie within. Let us meditate on God's promises, allowing them to take root in our souls and to blossom into a deeper trust in Him. And let us step out in faith, even when we're unsure of the path ahead, knowing that He is with us every step of the way.

The Power of Prayer in Overcoming Doubt

"Do not be anxious about anything, but in everything by prayer and supplication with thanksgiving let your requests be made known to God. And the peace of God, which surpasses all understanding, will guard your hearts and your minds in Christ Jesus." (Philippians 4:6-7, ESV).

In the labyrinth of doubt, where uncertainties twist and turn, prayer emerges as a guiding light, illuminating the path towards trust and surrender. It's the lifeline that connects us to the heart of God, a sacred space where we can pour out our anxieties, voice our questions, and find solace in His presence.

Prayer is not simply a religious ritual or a recitation of memorized words. It's an intimate conversation with the Creator of the universe, a chance to express our deepest longings, fears, and hopes. It's an invitation to come before God just as we are, with all our imperfections and vulnerabilities, trusting that He hears our every word and understands the depths of our hearts.

In moments of doubt, when our faith feels fragile and uncertain, prayer becomes a vital tool for strengthening our trust in God. It's a way of acknowledging our limitations, surrendering our anxieties to Him, and seeking His guidance and wisdom. Through prayer, we invite God to enter into our struggles, to illuminate the darkness with His light, and to lead us back to a place of peace and confidence.

The Bible is replete with examples of individuals who turned to prayer in times of doubt and uncertainty. David, the shepherd-king, poured out his heart to God in the Psalms, expressing his fears, his frustrations, and his unwavering trust in God's faithfulness. Jesus himself, in the Garden of Gethsemane, prayed fervently, seeking strength and guidance as He faced the cross. These examples remind us that prayer is not a sign of weakness but an act of courage, a willingness to acknowledge our dependence on God and to seek His help in navigating life's challenges.

When doubts arise, we can bring them before God in prayer, trusting that He is big enough to handle our questions and uncertainties. We can express our fears, our anxieties, and even our anger, knowing that He understands our human emotions and longs to comfort us in our distress. We can ask for wisdom, for clarity, and for the strength to trust in His plans, even when we don't fully understand them.

Prayer is not just about asking; it's also about listening. As we quiet our hearts and minds, we create space for God to speak to us. We may hear His voice through a gentle whisper, a sudden insight, or a deep sense of peace that washes over us. We may find answers to our questions, or we may simply receive the reassurance that God is with us, that He loves us, and that He will never leave us or forsake us.

The power of prayer lies not in its ability to change God's mind but in its ability to transform our own hearts. As we pour out our souls to Him, we surrender our anxieties and fears, allowing His peace to fill the empty spaces. We shift our focus from our own limitations to His limitless power and love. We find the courage to trust, even when the path ahead seems unclear, knowing that He is leading us towards a future filled with hope and purpose.

In the face of doubt and uncertainty, prayer is not a magic formula for instant solutions. It's a discipline, a practice that requires intentionality and perseverance. It's a way of cultivating a deeper relationship with God, one that is marked by honesty, vulnerability, and unwavering trust.

Developing a consistent prayer life

Establishing a routine for prayer can be a helpful first step in cultivating a consistent practice. Setting aside a specific time and place each day for prayer creates a sacred space for communion with God. It signals to our hearts and minds that this is a time of importance, a moment to set aside the distractions of the world and focus on our relationship with our Creator.

Whether it's early in the morning, during a lunch break, or before bed, find a time that works best for you and commit to it. Choose a quiet place where you can be alone with your thoughts and with God. It might be a corner of your bedroom, a peaceful spot in nature, or even a quiet chapel. The key is to create an environment that fosters focus and reflection, allowing you to fully engage in the act of prayer.

However, while routine can be helpful, it's important to remember that prayer is not confined to a specific time or place. It's a conversation with God that can happen anytime, anywhere. Whether you're driving to work, taking a walk, or simply going about your daily tasks, you can carry on an ongoing dialogue with Him.

Prayer is not limited to spoken words. It can also be expressed through writing, music, art, or even silence. Experiment with different forms of prayer to find what resonates most deeply with you. You might try writing your prayers in a journal, composing a song of praise, or simply sitting in quiet contemplation, allowing your heart to commune with God.

The key is to find a rhythm of prayer that feels natural and authentic to you. Don't be afraid to try new things, to step outside your comfort zone, and to explore different ways of connecting with God. The more you engage in prayer, the more you will discover its transformative power in your life.

Journaling your prayers can be a particularly helpful practice for those struggling with doubt and uncertainty. Writing down your thoughts and feelings can bring clarity and focus to your prayers, allowing you to articulate your concerns and anxieties more clearly. It can also serve as a record of your spiritual journey, documenting your growth and God's faithfulness over time.

As you journal your prayers, be honest and vulnerable. Pour out your heart to God, expressing your doubts, your fears, and your hopes. Ask Him for guidance, for strength, and for the courage to trust in His plans, even when you don't fully understand them. Remember, He already knows the depths of your heart; He longs for you to share them with Him openly and without fear.

Setting specific prayer goals can also be a helpful way to focus your prayers and track your progress. These goals might be related to specific areas of your life where you're struggling with trust, such as your relationships, your finances, or your health. They might also be broader goals, such as deepening your relationship with God, growing in your understanding of His Word, or developing a more consistent prayer life.

As you set your prayer goals, be realistic and specific. Instead of simply praying for "more faith," consider praying for the courage to trust God in a particular situation or for the wisdom to discern His will in a specific decision. Write down your goals and review them regularly, tracking your progress and celebrating answered prayers.

Remember, prayer is not a one-way street. It's a dialogue, a conversation with a loving and attentive God. As you pray, be sure to listen for His response. He may speak to you through a gentle whisper, a sudden insight, or a deep sense of peace that washes over you. He may answer your prayers directly, or He may lead you in a different direction than you anticipated. The key is to remain open to His guidance and to trust that He is working all things together for your good.

Developing a consistent prayer life takes time and effort, but it's a worthwhile investment in your spiritual well-being. As you make prayer a priority, you will find that your relationship with God deepens, your trust in Him grows stronger, and your doubts begin to fade. You will discover that prayer is not just a way of coping with uncertainty; it's a way of living in constant communion with the One who loves you unconditionally and who holds your future in His hands.

So, let us commit to cultivating a consistent prayer life, one that is marked by honesty, vulnerability, and unwavering trust. Let us set aside time each day to commune with God, to express our gratitude, to share our struggles, and to seek His guidance. And let us trust that as we draw near to Him in prayer, He will draw near to us, filling us with His peace, His strength, and His unfailing love.

Examples of prayers for reassurance

In the quest for reassurance amidst the storms of doubt, prayer becomes a sanctuary of solace and strength. It is the channel through which we pour out our hearts to God, expressing our fears, our questions, and our longing for His unwavering love. As we lift our voices in prayer, we invite Him to meet us in our vulnerability, to speak into our uncertainties, and to guide us towards a deeper trust in His promises.

One powerful way to pray for reassurance is to incorporate Scripture into our prayers. The Bible, a treasure trove of divine wisdom and comfort, offers countless verses that speak directly to our struggles and fears. By weaving these verses into our prayers, we root our petitions in the bedrock of God's unchanging truth, reminding ourselves of His faithfulness throughout history and His promises for our future.

When anxiety grips our hearts, we can pray, *"Lord, I am feeling anxious and overwhelmed. But Your Word reminds me that You will keep in perfect peace those whose minds are steadfast, because they trust in You. Help me to fix my mind on You, to trust in Your goodness, and to find peace in Your presence."* **(Isaiah 26:3, ESV)**

When doubts cloud our vision, we can pray, *"Lord, I am struggling to believe. But Your Word reminds me that faith is the assurance of things hoped for, the conviction of things not seen. Help me to see beyond my doubts, to trust in Your promises, and to walk by faith, not by sight."* **(Hebrews 11:1, ESV)**

When we feel lost and alone, we can pray, *"Lord, I feel so distant from You. But Your Word reminds me that You are near to the brokenhearted and save the crushed in spirit. Draw near to me, O Lord, and fill me with Your presence. Remind me that I am never alone, for You are always with me."* **(Psalm 34:18, ESV)**

These scriptural prayers, rooted in the timeless truths of God's Word, can be a source of immense comfort and reassurance. They remind us that we are not the first to grapple with doubt and uncertainty, and that God has a history of meeting His people in their moments of need. They also invite us to participate in the ongoing story of God's faithfulness, trusting that He will continue to fulfil His promises in our lives.

While scriptural prayers offer a powerful foundation for our communication with God, personalized prayers can also be a source of deep connection and healing. When we bring our specific struggles and concerns before God, we invite Him to intervene in our unique circumstances. We acknowledge that He knows us intimately, that He sees our pain, our fears, and our deepest longings.

If you're struggling with a difficult decision, you might pray, *"Lord, I'm facing a choice that fills me with uncertainty. Please guide me, give me wisdom, and show me the path that aligns with Your will for my life."* If you're grieving a loss, you might pray, *"God, my heart is broken, and I don't understand why this has happened. Please comfort me in my sorrow, give me strength to carry on, and help me to trust in Your goodness, even in the midst of this pain."*

These personalized prayers, born out of the depths of our hearts, create a space for authentic communication with God. They allow us to express our deepest emotions, to acknowledge our vulnerabilities, and to seek His guidance and comfort in the specific challenges we face. As we pour out our hearts to Him, we open ourselves to His transformative power, allowing Him to bring healing, peace, and a renewed sense of trust.

Praying in community can also be a powerful source of reassurance and strength. When we gather with other believers to lift our voices in prayer, we create a sacred space where doubts can be shared, burdens can be lifted, and faith can be amplified. We remind ourselves that we are not alone in our struggles, that countless others are walking a similar path.

In the presence of fellow believers, we witness the power of collective prayer, as individual petitions merge into a chorus of supplication and praise. We hear the affirmations of faith from others, their words echoing the promises of Scripture and reminding us of God's unwavering love. We experience the comfort of shared vulnerability, knowing that we can be honest about our doubts and fears without judgment or condemnation.

Finally, spontaneous prayer, born out of the overflow of our hearts, can be a source of profound connection with God. These unscripted prayers, uttered in moments of joy, sorrow, or simply quiet reflection, allow us to communicate with God in a raw and authentic way. We can express our gratitude for His blessings, cry out to Him in our pain, or simply bask in His presence, offering words of love and adoration.

Spontaneous prayer breaks down the barriers between us and God, inviting us to enter into a deeper level of intimacy with Him. It's a reminder that our relationship with Him is not confined to formal rituals or structured prayers; it's an ongoing conversation that can happen anytime, anywhere.

As you explore these different forms of prayer, remember that there is no right or wrong way to pray. The most important thing is to come before God with an open and honest heart, trusting that He hears your every word and longs to meet you in your vulnerability. Whether you're praying with Scripture, expressing your personal struggles, joining with others in community prayer, or simply pouring out your heart in spontaneous conversation, know that God is listening, and He is faithful to answer.

In the words of Jesus, *"Ask, and it will be given to you; seek, and you will find; knock, and it will be opened to you. For everyone who asks receives, and the one who seeks finds, and to the one who knocks it will be opened."* **(Matthew 7:7-8, ESV)**

.

Listening for God's guidance in prayer

"Be still, and know that I am God." **(Psalm 46:10, ESV).** In the stillness of prayer, we create a sacred space for listening, a sanctuary where the whispers of God's guidance can be heard amidst the clamour of our doubts and uncertainties. It's in these quiet moments of reflection that we open ourselves to His wisdom, allowing His peace to wash over us and His truth to illuminate our path.

Silence, often uncomfortable and unfamiliar in our fast-paced world, becomes a precious gift in prayer. It's an invitation to quiet the noise of our own thoughts and anxieties, to create a receptive space where God's voice can resonate within our hearts. As we cultivate a posture of stillness, we shift our focus from speaking to listening, from making requests to receiving guidance.

In the silence, we may experience a sense of anticipation, a waiting upon the Lord with expectant hearts. We may feel a deep peace settling over us, a calm assurance that transcends our circumstances. Or we may simply encounter the quiet presence of God, a gentle reminder that He is with us, even in the midst of our uncertainties.

As we continue to practice silence and reflection in prayer, we begin to develop a greater sensitivity to God's voice. We learn to discern His gentle whispers from the noise of our own thoughts, to distinguish His guidance from our own desires. This discernment is not an overnight process; it requires patience, practice, and a willingness to surrender our own agendas to His will.

God's voice may come in many forms. It may be a sense of peace that settles over us, a confirmation of a decision we've been wrestling with, or a subtle nudge in a particular direction. It may be a verse of Scripture that leaps off the page, speaking directly to our situation, or a word of encouragement from a trusted friend or mentor.

The key is to remain open and receptive to God's leading, trusting that He will speak to us in ways that we can understand. As we cultivate a posture of listening, we will find that His guidance becomes clearer and more consistent, providing a firm foundation for our faith in times of doubt.

Scripture reflection is another powerful tool for listening for God's guidance in prayer. As we meditate on His Word, allowing its truths to penetrate our hearts and minds, we open ourselves to His wisdom and direction. The Bible is filled with stories of individuals who faced challenges and uncertainties, yet ultimately found hope and strength in God's promises. Their experiences can offer valuable insights into our own struggles, reminding us that we are not alone and that God is faithful to guide and sustain us.

As you read and reflect on Scripture, pay attention to the verses that resonate with your current situation. What words of comfort or encouragement do they offer? What promises of God's faithfulness do they reveal? How can you apply these truths to your own life, allowing them to shape your thoughts, your actions, and your relationship with God?

In addition to individual reflection, seeking counsel from trusted mentors or friends can also be a helpful way to discern God's guidance. As we share our doubts and uncertainties with others, we invite them to join us in prayer, to offer their own insights and perspectives, and to help us see our situation from a different angle. Their wisdom and encouragement can be a source of clarity and reassurance, helping us to navigate the complexities of faith with greater confidence.

Remember, listening for God's guidance is not a passive activity. It requires intentionality, humility, and a willingness to surrender our own agendas to His will. It's about creating space for Him to speak, trusting that He will lead us in the way we should go. As we cultivate a posture of listening, we will find that our faith deepens, our trust in God grows stronger, and our doubts begin to fade. We will discover that even in the midst of uncertainty, we can rest in the assurance that He is with us, guiding us, and leading us towards a future filled with hope and purpose.

Community Support: Strengthening Each Other's Faith

"Two are better than one, because they have a good reward for their toil. For if they fall, one will lift up his fellow. But woe to him who is alone when he falls and has not another to lift him up!" (Ecclesiastes 4:9-10, ESV)

In the journey of faith, we are not meant to walk alone. The Christian community, a tapestry of diverse individuals united by a shared belief in Christ, offers a powerful source of support, encouragement, and strength. Within this tapestry, we find solace in times of doubt, encouragement in moments of weakness, and the collective strength to overcome the challenges that threaten to derail our trust in God.

The image of a fragile and easily broken single thread stands in stark contrast to the interwoven strength of a tapestry. Each thread, though seemingly insignificant on its own, contributes to the overall beauty and resilience of the whole. Similarly, within the Christian community, each individual, with their unique gifts and experiences, plays a vital role in supporting and strengthening the faith of others.

When doubts arise, when uncertainties cloud our vision, the community becomes a safe haven where we can express our fears and questions without judgment or condemnation. It's a place where we can find solace in the shared experiences of others, recognizing that we are not alone in our struggles. It's a space where we can receive encouragement and support, reminding us of God's faithfulness and His promises for our lives.

Imagine a group of friends gathered around a table, sharing their stories of doubt and faith. One person speaks of a recent loss that has shaken their belief in God's goodness. Another shares their struggle to reconcile the complexities of the world with the simplicity of their faith. And yet another expresses their fear of the future, unsure of what lies ahead.

As each person shares their heart, a sense of connection and understanding fills the room. The weight of individual burdens is lifted, replaced by a shared sense of hope and resilience. In the presence of others who have walked a similar path, doubts lose their power, and faith begins to rekindle.

The Christian community offers more than just a listening ear; it provides a network of support and accountability. When we are struggling to trust, we can turn to trusted mentors or spiritual leaders for guidance and wisdom. We can join small groups or prayer circles where we can share our burdens and receive encouragement from fellow believers. We can participate in worship services and community events, reminding ourselves that we are part of something bigger than ourselves, a body of Christ that transcends our individual doubts and fears.

This collective support is not just a feel-good experience; it has a profound impact on our spiritual well-being. Studies have shown that individuals who are actively involved in a faith community tend to have stronger mental and emotional health, greater resilience in the face of adversity, and a deeper sense of purpose and meaning in their lives. They also report higher levels of trust in God and a greater sense of connection to something larger than themselves.

The Bible itself emphasizes the importance of community in the life of a believer. In Hebrews 10:24-25, we are encouraged to "consider how to stir up one another to love and good works, not neglecting to meet together, as is the habit of some, but encouraging one another, and all the more as you see the Day drawing near." This passage reminds us that we are not meant to live in isolation but to gather together, to encourage one another, and to spur one another on towards love and good deeds.

In the context of doubt and uncertainty, the Christian community becomes even more crucial. It provides a safe space for questioning, a supportive environment for growth, and a collective witness to God's faithfulness. It reminds us that we are not alone, that others have walked this path before us, and that together, we can overcome the challenges that threaten to derail our faith.

As you seek to embrace God's guidance amidst skepticism and uncertainty, don't underestimate the power of community. Surround yourself with people who will uplift and encourage you, who will challenge you to grow in your faith, and who will walk alongside you through the valleys of doubt. Remember, we are stronger together than we are alone. In the collective strength of the Christian community, we find the courage to trust, the resilience to persevere, and the unwavering hope that anchors our souls in the midst of life's storms.

Finding Supportive Faith Groups

Within the embrace of a supportive faith community, we discover a haven where our doubts and uncertainties are met with understanding, encouragement, and a shared commitment to seeking God's truth. It's a place where we can journey together, drawing strength from one another's experiences, and finding reassurance in the collective pursuit of a deeper trust in God.

The Christian community, like a vibrant mosaic, comprises a multitude of groups and ministries, each offering a unique expression of faith and a distinct avenue for spiritual growth. From small groups that meet in homes to church-wide ministries focused on specific needs, there are countless opportunities to connect with others who share your journey.

Some groups may focus on Bible study and theological exploration, offering a space for intellectual engagement with the complexities of faith. Others may emphasize prayer and worship, providing an atmosphere of spiritual renewal and connection with God. Still others may prioritize service and outreach, offering opportunities to put faith into action and make a tangible difference in the world.

The diversity of faith groups within the Christian community allows individuals to find their spiritual home, a place where they feel understood, accepted, and supported. It also provides opportunities to encounter faith expressed in different ways, enriching our own understanding of God's love and grace.

Finding a supportive faith group may involve some exploration and trial and error. Start by checking with your local church or denomination to see what groups or ministries they offer. Ask friends or family members for recommendations, or consider joining an online community or social media group focused on your specific interests or needs.

When evaluating potential groups, look for those that foster an atmosphere of openness and acceptance. The ideal group will be a safe space where you can express your doubts and questions without fear of judgment or condemnation. It will be a place where you feel comfortable sharing your struggles and celebrating your victories, knowing that you are surrounded by people who genuinely care about your spiritual well-being.

Within these groups, mentors can play a crucial role in helping individuals navigate their doubts and uncertainties. A mentor is someone who has walked the path of faith before you, someone who has wrestled with their own questions and emerged with a deeper trust in God. They can offer guidance, wisdom, and encouragement, helping you to see your struggles in a new light and to find hope in God's promises.

Mentorship is not about providing easy answers or dismissing your doubts. It's about walking alongside you on your journey, offering support, challenge, and accountability. A good mentor will listen to your concerns with empathy and understanding, point you to relevant Scripture passages, and encourage you to engage in practices that will strengthen your faith. They will also share their own stories of doubt and faith, reminding you that you are not alone and that God is faithful to meet us in our moments of need.

Engaging in service within a faith community can also be a powerful way to strengthen your trust in God. When we serve others, we put our faith into action, demonstrating love and compassion in tangible ways. This active expression of faith can be a source of profound joy and fulfillment, reminding us of the transformative power of God's love in our lives.

Service can also provide a much-needed perspective shift in times of doubt. When we focus on meeting the needs of others, we are less likely to become consumed by our own anxieties and uncertainties. We see the world through a lens of compassion, recognizing the pain and suffering of those around us and seeking to bring hope and healing to their lives.

Moreover, engaging in service alongside other believers can foster a deep sense of connection and unity. As we work together towards a common goal, we experience the power of collective action and the joy of shared purpose. We see first-hand how God can use ordinary people to accomplish extraordinary things, and we are reminded that we are part of something much larger than ourselves.

Within the fabric of the Christian fellowship, every strand is essential. If your pursuit involves scholarly discourse, rejuvenation of the spirit, or hands-on ministry, you'll find an assembly or outreach suited to your requirements, ready to assist you along your spiritual path. Engaging with a nurturing religious congregation fosters a web of connections that uphold you during periods of uncertainty, bolster you during lapses of strength, and embolden you to embody your beliefs with fortitude and assurance.

Remember, you are not alone. Countless others are walking a similar path, wrestling with similar questions, and seeking to deepen their trust in God. By connecting with them, sharing your struggles, and supporting one another, you can experience the transformative power of community and discover the joy of walking together in faith.

Sharing Testimonies of Trust and Doubt

Within the shelter of a loving and supportive faith community, we discover a sacred space where vulnerability is not a weakness but a catalyst for connection and growth. It is within this embrace that we can share our stories of doubt and faith, weaving together a tapestry of shared experiences that speaks to the universal human struggle to trust in God.

"Therefore encourage one another and build one another up, just as you are doing." (1 Thessalonians 5:11, ESV)

The apostle Paul's exhortation echoes through the ages, reminding us that the Christian life is not meant to be lived in isolation. We are called to come alongside one another, to offer encouragement, and to build each other up in faith. Sharing our testimonies of trust and doubt is a powerful way to fulfill this calling, creating a space where vulnerability is honored and authenticity is celebrated.

When we open our hearts and share our stories, we create a ripple effect of empathy and understanding. We discover that we are not alone in our struggles, that others have walked a similar path, wrestling with the same questions and uncertainties. This shared experience can be incredibly validating, reminding us that doubt is not a sign of weakness or a lack of faith, but a natural part of the human journey towards God.

Moreover, hearing how others have navigated their own doubts and emerged with a deeper trust in God can be a source of immense hope and encouragement. Their stories become beacons of light, illuminating the path for those who are still stumbling in the darkness. They remind us that even in the midst of our deepest struggles, God is still at work, weaving a tapestry of redemption and restoration.

Testimonies of faith, particularly those that acknowledge the presence of doubt, can also serve as powerful reminders of God's faithfulness. When we hear how others have experienced His love and guidance, even in the face of overwhelming challenges, it strengthens our own resolve to trust in Him. We see that He is not a distant deity but a loving Father who is intimately involved in our lives, working all things together for our good.

Creating safe spaces for sharing these testimonies is crucial. It's important to foster an environment where individuals feel comfortable opening up about their struggles without fear of judgment or condemnation. This may involve establishing ground rules for confidentiality and respect, ensuring that everyone feels heard and valued. It may also require intentional efforts to cultivate an atmosphere of grace and understanding, where vulnerability is met with empathy and encouragement.

Regular sharing times during group meetings or gatherings can provide a structured opportunity for individuals to share their testimonies. These times can be facilitated by a leader who creates a safe and welcoming space for open dialogue. It's important to emphasize that sharing is not mandatory; individuals should feel free to participate at their own pace and comfort level.

Encouraging authenticity in these testimonies is also essential. When we share our stories with honesty and vulnerability, we create deeper connections with others and foster a greater sense of trust within the community. We move beyond superficial platitudes and delve into the raw and real experiences of faith, allowing God to use our stories to touch the hearts of others.

The act of sharing itself can be a form of healing and growth. As we articulate our struggles and triumphs, we gain a clearer understanding of our own faith journey. We see how God has been at work in our lives, even in the midst of our doubts and uncertainties. We also experience the release that comes from sharing our burdens with others, allowing them to carry some of the weight and offer their support.

Moreover, sharing testimonies can create a culture of encouragement and accountability within the community. When we witness others' growth and transformation, it inspires us to persevere in our own faith journey. We see that doubt is not a dead end but a pathway to deeper trust and a more authentic relationship with God. We are reminded that we are all in this together, walking hand-in-hand towards a future filled with hope and purpose.

As you engage in the practice of sharing testimonies, remember that your story matters. Your experiences of doubt and faith, your struggles and triumphs, have the power to touch the hearts of others and to point them towards the unwavering love of God. Don't be afraid to open up, to be vulnerable, and to share your journey with those who will listen with compassion and understanding.

In the words of the apostle Peter, ***"But you are a chosen race, a royal priesthood, a holy nation, a people for his own possession, that you may proclaim the excellencies of him who called you out of darkness into his marvelous light."*** **(1 Peter 2:9, ESV)** Your testimony is a powerful tool for proclaiming God's goodness and inviting others to experience His transformative love.

So, let us create spaces within our faith communities where vulnerability is celebrated and authenticity is embraced. Let us share our stories of doubt and faith, encouraging one another and building each other up in love. And let us trust that as we do so, God will use our collective witness to draw others into His embrace, illuminating the path towards a deeper trust in His promises.

Encouraging Accountability Partnerships

"Iron sharpens iron, and one man sharpens another." (Proverbs 27:17, ESV). In the journey of faith, we are not meant to walk alone. We need companions who will challenge us, encourage us, and hold us accountable as we strive to deepen our trust in God. Accountability partnerships, rooted in mutual support and

encouragement, can be a powerful tool for overcoming doubt and cultivating a more resilient faith.

Accountability, in the context of faith, is not about judgment or condemnation. It's about creating a safe and supportive space where we can share our struggles, celebrate our victories, and spur one another on towards spiritual growth. It's about walking alongside one another, offering encouragement, guidance, and gentle reminders of God's truth.

When we enter into an accountability partnership, we commit to being honest and transparent about our faith journey. We share our doubts and fears, our hopes and dreams, and our ongoing efforts to live out our faith in the world. We invite another person into the sacred space of our spiritual lives, trusting that they will walk alongside us with compassion, understanding, and unwavering support.

Establishing an effective accountability partnership requires intentionality and commitment. It's important to choose a partner who is at a similar stage in their faith journey, someone who understands your struggles and can relate to your experiences. It's also helpful to set clear expectations and goals for the partnership. What specific areas of your faith do you want to focus on? How often will you meet or communicate? What kind of support and encouragement do you need from your partner?

Regular check-ins are essential for maintaining momentum and accountability. These check-ins can be in person, over the phone, or even through video calls. During these times, you can share your progress, discuss any challenges you're facing, and pray for one another. You can also study Scripture together, delve into spiritual books or resources, and encourage one another to put your faith into action.

Building trust is a crucial element of any successful accountability partnership. It's important to create an environment where both partners feel safe and valued, where they can be honest about their struggles without fear of judgment or condemnation. This requires open communication, active listening, and a genuine desire to see each other grow in faith.

As trust deepens, you'll find that your accountability partnership becomes a source of strength and encouragement. You'll have someone to celebrate your victories with, to offer support in times of difficulty, and to challenge you to step outside your comfort zone. You'll also have the opportunity to be that same source of support for your partner, walking alongside them as they navigate their own faith journey.

Celebrating progress together is an important aspect of accountability. When we acknowledge and affirm each other's spiritual milestones, we create a sense of shared accomplishment and motivation. We remind each other that growth is possible, even in the midst of doubt and uncertainty. We also reinforce the truth that God is at work in our lives, transforming us from the inside out.

As you reflect on your own faith journey, consider the role of accountability in your life. Do you have someone you can trust to walk alongside you, to offer support and encouragement, and to hold you accountable for living out your faith? If not, prayerfully consider seeking out an accountability partner. It could be a friend, a family member, a mentor, or even a pastor or counselor.

Remember, the Christian life is not meant to be lived in isolation. We need the support and encouragement of others to help us navigate the challenges of faith. By entering into an accountability partnership, we create a space for mutual growth, shared vulnerability, and a deeper connection with God. We discover that in the strength of community, we find the courage to trust, the resilience to persevere, and the unwavering hope that anchors our souls in the midst of life's storms.

Learning from Biblical Figures Who Faced Doubt

In the vast library of human experience contained within the Bible, we find stories that echo across the ages, touching the deepest chords of our hearts and illuminating the complexities of faith. Among these narratives are the tales of individuals who, despite their deep devotion to God, wrestled with doubt, fear, and uncertainty. Their struggles, preserved in the Bible, offer a profound source of comfort and guidance for those who find themselves grappling with similar challenges today.

In these stories, we encounter men and women who questioned God's plans, doubted His promises, and even expressed anger and frustration in the face of adversity. We see them wrestling with their limitations, grappling with the mysteries of faith, and seeking to reconcile their experiences with their understanding of God's character. Their honesty and vulnerability, preserved in the pages of Scripture, remind us that doubt is not a sign of weakness or a lack of faith; it is a natural part of the human experience, even within the context of a deep and abiding relationship with God.

By exploring these stories, we gain valuable insights into the nature of doubt and its role in our spiritual journeys. We see how doubt can be a catalyst for growth, prompting us to seek a deeper understanding of God and His ways.

We witness how individuals wrestled with their questions, engaged in honest conversations with God, and ultimately emerged with a stronger, more resilient faith. Their experiences offer us hope and encouragement, reminding us that we are not alone in our struggles and that God is faithful to meet us in our moments of uncertainty.

These biblical narratives also provide a framework for understanding the different faces of doubt. We see individuals wrestling with intellectual doubts, questioning the validity of their beliefs or the existence of God. We witness emotional doubts, rooted in fear, anxiety, or past traumas. And we encounter existential doubts, those deep-seated questions about the meaning and purpose of life.

By examining these diverse expressions of doubt, we can better understand our own struggles and identify the root causes of our skepticism. We can learn from the mistakes and triumphs of those who have gone before us, gleaning wisdom from their experiences and applying their lessons to our own lives.

Furthermore, the stories of biblical figures who faced doubt offer a powerful reminder that God is not intimidated by our questions or our uncertainties. He welcomes our honesty and vulnerability, inviting us to bring our whole selves before Him, even the parts that are filled with doubt and fear. In fact, He often uses these very struggles to draw us closer to Him, to deepen our relationship with Him, and to reveal His love and faithfulness in new and profound ways.

So, let us turn to the stories of those who faced doubt, not with fear or trepidation, but with a sense of curiosity and expectation. Let us learn from their experiences, draw inspiration from their resilience, and find hope in their unwavering trust in God. And let us remember that we are part of a long and storied tradition of faith, a community of believers who have wrestled with doubt throughout the ages and emerged with a deeper understanding of God's love and grace.

Jacob Wrestling with God

In the Old Testament there is a story that resonates with the timeless human struggle to reconcile faith with uncertainty. It's the story of Jacob, a man marked by both ambition and vulnerability, who found himself wrestling with God on the banks of the Jabbok River. This encounter, shrouded in mystery and symbolism, speaks volumes about the complexities of faith and the transformative power of wrestling with doubt.

Under the cloak of night, Jacob, alone and burdened by the weight of his past choices, encounters a mysterious figure. A struggle ensues, a physical and spiritual wrestling match that lasts until daybreak. Jacob, clinging to his opponent with unwavering determination, refuses to let go until he receives a blessing.

This dramatic encounter serves as a powerful metaphor for the spiritual struggles we all face. It's a picture of our own wrestling with God, our desperate pleas for answers, our yearning for reassurance in the face of uncertainty.

Jacob's refusal to let go, even in the face of pain and exhaustion, reflects the tenacity of the human spirit, our relentless pursuit of meaning and connection with the divine.

But this story is not just about struggle; it's also about transformation. As the sun rises, Jacob emerges from the encounter with a new name, Israel, meaning "he who struggles with God." This change of identity signifies a profound shift in his understanding of himself and his relationship with God. He is no longer simply Jacob, the deceiver, the one who wrestled with his brother for the birthright. He is now Israel, the one who has wrestled with God and prevailed.

This transformation highlights the potential for growth and renewal that lies within the crucible of doubt. When we wrestle with God, when we bring our questions and uncertainties before Him, we open ourselves to the possibility of change. We allow Him to reshape our identities, to refine our understanding, and to lead us into a deeper experience of His love and grace.

But the story doesn't end there. As Jacob limps away from the encounter, bearing the physical marks of his struggle, he receives a blessing from God. This blessing, a tangible sign of God's favor and acceptance, underscores a crucial truth: our wrestling with God does not disqualify us from His love; it can, in fact, lead to a deeper and more intimate relationship with Him.

God sees our struggles, He hears our cries, and He values our honesty and vulnerability. He welcomes our wrestling as a path to understanding and growth. He is not threatened by our questions or our doubts; He invites us to bring them before Him, trusting that He will meet us in our uncertainties and lead us into a deeper experience of His truth.

The story of Jacob wrestling with God challenges the notion that faith must be devoid of struggle. It reminds us that doubt is not an anomaly but an integral part of the human experience, even within the context of a deep and abiding relationship with God. It encourages us to embrace our questions, to engage in honest conversations with Him, and to trust that He will meet us in the midst of our wrestling.

As you reflect on your own journey of faith, consider the moments when you have wrestled with God. What questions have you brought before Him? What fears and uncertainties have you expressed? How has He met you in those moments, offering guidance, comfort, and a renewed sense of purpose?

Abraham's journey of faith

The In the annals of faith, Abraham stands as a towering figure, his journey etched into the heart of Scripture as a testament to the transformative power of trust in God. Yet, his path was not one of unwavering certainty; it was a winding road marked by moments of doubt, questioning, and profound challenges. His story, however, offers us a profound source of inspiration and guidance as we navigate our own struggles with trust and uncertainty.

The narrative begins with a bold call and a seemingly impossible promise. God summons Abraham, then known as Abram, to leave his homeland and venture into the unknown, assuring him that he will become a great nation and a blessing to all the families of the earth. This call, while exhilarating, is also fraught with uncertainty. Abraham must leave behind the familiar comforts of his home, his family, and his cultural identity, trusting in a promise that seems far-fetched and improbable.

His journey is a testament to the importance of stepping out in faith, even when the path ahead is unclear. It's a reminder that God often calls us to venture beyond our comfort zones, to embrace the unknown, and to trust in His guidance, even when it seems counterintuitive or even impossible.

As Abraham embarks on this journey, he encounters numerous challenges that test his faith and patience. Years pass, and the promised son, the heir to the covenant, remains elusive. Sarah, his wife, grows old and barren, and doubts begin to creep into Abraham's heart. Will God truly fulfill His promise? Can he truly become the father of a great nation?

This prolonged period of waiting serves as a mirror for our own experiences. We, too, often find ourselves caught in the tension between God's promises and the realities of our circumstances. We pray for healing, for provision, for guidance, and yet the answers seem slow in coming. Doubts arise, whispering that perhaps God has forgotten us, or that His promises are not meant for us.

Abraham's story reminds us that waiting is an integral part of the faith journey. It's a time of testing, a crucible where our trust in God is refined and strengthened. It's also an opportunity to deepen our relationship with Him, to seek His presence more intentionally, and to learn to rely on His strength rather than our own.

In the midst of Abraham's waiting, God establishes a covenant with him, a solemn agreement that seals His promises and guarantees their fulfillment. This covenant, marked by the sign of circumcision, becomes a tangible reminder of God's faithfulness. It's a testament to His unwavering commitment to Abraham and his descendants, a promise that transcends time and circumstance.

The covenant serves as an anchor for Abraham's faith, a source of reassurance in the face of ongoing uncertainty. It reminds him that God's promises are not empty words; they are backed by His very character and His unwavering love. This covenant also foreshadows the ultimate covenant that God would establish through Jesus Christ, a covenant of grace and redemption that extends to all who believe.

The culmination of Abraham's journey of faith is perhaps the most challenging and awe-inspiring moment in his story. God calls him to sacrifice his beloved son, Isaac, the very fulfillment of the promise He had made years earlier. This test of faith pushes Abraham to the brink, forcing him to confront the deepest fears and uncertainties of his heart.

Yet, in a moment of profound obedience, Abraham prepares to offer Isaac as a sacrifice, trusting that God will provide a way, even if it means raising Isaac from the dead. His willingness to surrender his most precious possession to God demonstrates the ultimate expression of trust, a willingness to obey even when it seems incomprehensible or even unjust.

This pivotal moment in Abraham's story challenges us to examine our own responses to God's call. Are we willing to surrender our own desires and agendas to His will, even when it requires sacrifice or a leap of faith? Are we willing to trust Him, even when the path ahead seems uncertain or even painful?

Abraham's unwavering obedience, even in the face of unimaginable loss, is a testament to the transformative power of trust in God. It's a reminder that true faith is not about blind acceptance or passive resignation; it's about an active surrender to God's will, a willingness to follow Him wherever He leads, even when it challenges our understanding or tests the limits of our comfort.

As we reflect on Abraham's journey of faith, we are invited to embrace the complexities of our own struggles with trust. We are reminded that doubt is not a barrier to faith but an opportunity for deeper engagement with God. We are encouraged to step out in faith, even when the path ahead is unclear, trusting that He will guide us and provide for us every step of the way. And we are challenged to cultivate a radical obedience, a willingness to surrender our own desires and agendas to His perfect will.

In the words of the apostle Paul, ***"By faith Abraham obeyed when he was called to go out to a place that he was to receive as an inheritance. And he went out, not knowing where he was going." (Hebrews 11:8, ESV)*** May we, like Abraham, have the courage to embrace the unknown, to trust in God's promises, and to walk boldly in faith, even when the path ahead seems uncertain.

Job's endurance through suffering

The echoes of Abraham's unwavering obedience and Jacob's transformative wrestling match reverberate through the corridors of faith, reminding us that doubt, while a formidable adversary, can be a catalyst for profound spiritual growth. But it is in the crucible of suffering, where questions burn brightest and trust feels most fragile, that we find perhaps the most poignant testament to the enduring power of faith. This is where we turn to the story of Job, a man whose steadfastness in the face of unimaginable loss speaks volumes to those who grapple with doubt and uncertainty today.

Job, a righteous and prosperous man, is suddenly plunged into a maelstrom of suffering. He loses his wealth, his children, and his health, his once-comfortable life reduced to ashes. In the depths of his despair, he cries out to God, questioning His justice, His goodness, and even His very presence. His lamentations, raw and unfiltered, echo the cries of countless hearts throughout history who have grappled with the seeming senselessness of suffering.

"Why did I not die at birth, come forth from the womb and expire? Why were there knees to receive me, or breasts for me to suck? For then I would have lain down and been quiet; I would have slept; then I would have been at rest." (Job 3:11-13, ESV). Job's words, filled with anguish and despair, give voice to the questions that often arise in the face of tragedy and loss. We, too, may find ourselves questioning God's plans, wondering why He allows suffering to touch our lives or the lives of those we love.

Yet, even in his darkest hour, Job refuses to curse God or abandon his faith. He clings to the belief that God is ultimately good and just, even when His ways are beyond our comprehension. His unwavering loyalty, even in the face of unimaginable suffering, is a testament to the enduring power of faith, a reminder that even in the depths of despair, we can still find hope and strength in God's presence.

As Job wrestles with his questions and doubts, his friends offer him a series of well-intentioned but ultimately misguided explanations for his suffering. They suggest that he must have sinned, that his misfortune is a punishment for some hidden transgression. Their words, while meant to comfort, only serve to deepen Job's pain and isolation. They highlight the danger of seeking answers in the wrong places, of relying on human wisdom rather than divine revelation.

Job's friends, in their eagerness to provide explanations, fail to truly listen to his pain. They offer platitudes and clichés instead of empathy and understanding. Their approach serves as a cautionary tale for us, reminding us to be mindful of how we respond to those who are suffering. Instead of offering quick fixes or simplistic answers, we should strive to create a safe space where individuals can express their doubts and questions without fear of judgment or condemnation. We should offer a listening ear, a compassionate heart, and a gentle reminder of God's unwavering love.

In the climax of the story, Job finally encounters God. He demands an audience with his Creator, determined to receive answers to his questions and to understand the reasons for his suffering. God's response is not what Job expects. Instead of providing a detailed explanation, God reveals His power and majesty, His sovereignty over creation, and His infinite wisdom.

"Where were you when I laid the foundation of the earth? Tell me, if you have understanding. Who determined its measurements—surely you know! Or

who stretched the line upon it? On what were its bases sunk, or who laid its cornerstone, when the morning stars sang together and all the sons of God shouted for joy?" (Job 38:4-7, ESV). God's questions, though seemingly rhetorical, challenge Job to acknowledge the limitations of his own understanding. They remind him that God's ways are higher than our ways, His thoughts higher than our thoughts.

This encounter with God, though not providing the answers Job sought, leads to a profound transformation in his perspective. He recognizes the futility of trying to comprehend the mysteries of God's will and instead chooses to trust in His goodness and sovereignty. *"I know that you can do all things, and that no purpose of yours can be thwarted." (Job 42:2, ESV).*

Job's story culminates in a beautiful picture of restoration and hope. God blesses him with twice as much as he had before, restoring his health, his wealth, and his family. This restoration is not simply a reward for his faithfulness; it's a testament to God's redemptive power, His ability to bring beauty from ashes and to turn mourning into dancing.

As we reflect on Job's endurance through suffering, we are reminded that doubt and faith can coexist. We can question God's plans while still trusting in His goodness. We can lament our losses while still clinging to the hope of His promises. And we can endure through trials, knowing that He is with us, even in the darkest valleys.

Job's story offers a powerful message of hope for those who are struggling with doubt and uncertainty. It reminds us that God is not distant or indifferent to our pain. He sees our tears, He hears our cries, and He longs to comfort us in our distress. It also assures us that He is able to bring good out of even the most difficult circumstances, that He can redeem our suffering and use it for His glory.

So, let us take courage from Job's example. Let us not be afraid to bring our questions and doubts before God, trusting that He can handle our honesty and vulnerability. Let us persevere in faith, even when the path ahead seems dark and uncertain, knowing that He is with us, guiding us, and leading us towards a future filled with hope and restoration.

Practical Steps for Building Faith

"Faith comes from hearing, and hearing through the word of Christ." (Romans 10:17, ESV).

This verse encapsulates a fundamental truth: faith is not a static state, but a dynamic process that requires nourishment and cultivation. It's a muscle that grows stronger through exercise, a flame that burns brighter with the addition of fuel. In the face of doubt and uncertainty, we can actively build our faith by engaging in everyday practices that draw us closer to God and deepen our trust in His promises.

Just as a healthy body requires regular exercise and nutritious food, a healthy faith requires intentional practices that feed our souls and strengthen our connection with God. These practices are not meant to be burdensome or legalistic; they are invitations to encounter God's presence, to experience His love, and to grow in our understanding of His truth.

One of the most powerful ways to build faith is through consistent engagement with Scripture. The Bible, a treasure trove of divine wisdom and guidance, offers a wealth of resources for navigating the complexities of life and faith. As we read and meditate on its pages, we encounter stories of individuals who wrestled with their own doubts and fears, yet ultimately found solace and strength in God's unwavering love and faithfulness.

We also encounter the very words of God, spoken through prophets, poets, and apostles, revealing His character, His promises, and His plans for our lives. These words, when internalized and applied, have the power to transform our hearts and minds, shaping our beliefs, our attitudes, and our actions.

In addition to reading the Bible, there are countless other spiritual practices that can help us build faith and cultivate trust in God. Prayer, as we've already explored, is a vital means of communicating with God, expressing our gratitude, sharing our burdens, and seeking His guidance. Worship, whether through music, singing, or other forms of creative expression, allows us to connect with God on a deeper level, offering our hearts and minds in adoration and praise.

Silence and solitude, often overlooked in our busy lives, can also be powerful tools for spiritual growth. In the quietness, we create space for God to speak to our hearts, to reveal His truth, and to guide us in the way we should go. It's in these moments of stillness that we can truly listen for His voice, discerning His whispers from the noise of our own thoughts and anxieties.

Serving others, both within the church community and in the wider world, is another way to put our faith into action and experience God's love in a tangible way. When we reach out to those in need, offering compassion, support, and practical assistance, we become conduits of God's grace, reflecting His love to a hurting world. This act of service not only blesses others but also strengthens our own faith, reminding us of the transformative power of God's love in our lives.

Finally, surrounding ourselves with a supportive community of believers is essential for building faith and overcoming doubt. In the company of others who share our beliefs and values, we find encouragement, accountability, and a sense of belonging. We can share our struggles openly, knowing that we will be met with understanding and support. We can also learn from the experiences of others, gaining wisdom and insights that can help us navigate our own faith journey.

As you embark on this journey of building faith, remember that it's not about achieving perfection or eliminating all doubts. It's about cultivating a deeper relationship with God, one that is marked by trust, surrender, and a willingness to grow. It's about embracing the practices that nourish your soul and draw you closer to Him, even in the midst of uncertainty.

Daily devotionals and reflections

The journey towards deeper trust in God is often paved with moments of quiet reflection and intentional seeking. Over the next 30 days, let these questions and meditations guide you as you explore the depths of your heart and encounter the unwavering love of your Heavenly Father. May each day bring you closer to a place of peace, understanding, and renewed faith.

DAY 1

"This is the day that the Lord has made; let us rejoice and be glad in it." (Psalm 118:24, ESV) How can I incorporate gratitude into my daily devotional time, even when facing doubts?

_____

_____

_____

_____

_____

_____

_____

_____

_____

_____

_____

DAY 2

"But seek first the kingdom of God and his righteousness, and all these things will be added to you." (Matthew 6:33, ESV) In what ways can I prioritize my relationship with God through daily devotionals, even amidst a busy schedule?

_____

_____

_____

_____

_____

_____

_____

_____

_____

_____

_____

_____

DAY 3

"**Do not be conformed to this world, but be transformed by the renewal of your mind, that by testing you may discern what is the will of God, what is good and acceptable and perfect." (Romans 12:2, ESV)** How can daily reflection on Scripture help me reshape my thoughts and align them with God's truth?

_____
_____
_____
_____
_____
_____
_____
_____
_____
_____
_____
_____
_____

DAY 4

"For the word of God is living and active, sharper than any two-edged sword, piercing to the division of soul and of spirit, of joints and of marrow, and discerning the thoughts and intentions of the heart." (Hebrews 4:12, ESV) In what ways can engaging with Scripture during my devotionals challenge me to confront my doubts and deepen my faith?

_____
_____
_____
_____
_____
_____
_____
_____
_____
_____
_____
_____

DAY 5

"**Let the word of Christ dwell in you richly, teaching and admonishing one another in all wisdom, singing psalms and hymns and spiritual songs, with thankfulness in your hearts to God.**" **(Colossians 3:16, ESV)** How can I allow God's Word to permeate my thoughts and actions throughout the day, even after my devotional time is over?

_____

_____

_____

_____

_____

_____

_____

_____

_____

_____

_____

_____

DAY 6

"I can do all things through him who strengthens me." (Philippians 4:13, ESV) How can I draw strength from God's promises during my devotional time, especially when facing challenges or uncertainties?

_____
_____
_____
_____
_____
_____
_____
_____
_____
_____
_____
_____

DAY 7

"Cast all your anxiety on him because he cares for you." (1 Peter 5:7, ESV) In what ways can I surrender my worries and anxieties to God during my devotional time, allowing Him to carry my burdens?

_____
_____
_____
_____
_____
_____
_____
_____
_____
_____
_____
_____

DAY 8

"The Lord is near to all who call on him, to all who call on him in truth." (Psalm 145:18, ESV) How can I cultivate a sense of intimacy with God through prayer and reflection during my devotionals?

_____
_____
_____
_____
_____
_____
_____
_____
_____
_____
_____
_____

DAY 9

"And without faith it is impossible to please him, for whoever would draw near to God must believe that he exists and that he rewards those who seek him." (Hebrews 11:6, ESV) How can my daily devotional practice strengthen my belief in God's existence and His desire to connect with me?

_____
_____
_____
_____
_____
_____
_____
_____
_____
_____
_____
_____
_____

DAY 10

"Rejoice always, pray without ceasing, give thanks in all circumstances; for this is the will of God in Christ Jesus for you." (1 Thessalonians 5:16-18, ESV) How can I cultivate a spirit of joy, gratitude, and constant prayer throughout my day, even when facing challenges?

_____

_____

_____

_____

_____

_____

_____

_____

_____

_____

_____

_____

_____

DAY 11

"**Finally, brothers, whatever is true, whatever is honorable, whatever is just, whatever is pure, whatever is lovely, whatever is commendable, if there is any excellence, if there is anything worthy of praise, think about these things." (Philippians 4:8, ESV)** How can I use my devotional time to focus on the positive aspects of my life and faith, even when doubts arise?

_____

_____

_____

_____

_____

_____

_____

_____

_____

_____

_____

DAY 12

"But grow in the grace and knowledge of our Lord and Savior Jesus Christ. To him be the glory both now and to the day of eternity. Amen." (2 Peter 3:18, ESV) How can my daily devotionals help me grow in my understanding of God's grace and the person of Jesus Christ?

_____

_____

_____

_____

_____

_____

_____

_____

_____

_____

_____

DAY 13

"For we walk by faith, not by sight." (2 Corinthians 5:7, ESV) How can I use my devotional time to strengthen my faith and trust in God, even when I can't see the way forward?

_____
_____
_____
_____
_____
_____
_____
_____
_____
_____
_____
_____
_____
_____

DAY 14

"**The steadfast love of the Lord never ceases; his mercies never come to an end; they are new every morning; great is your faithfulness.**" **(Lamentations 3:22-23, ESV)** How can reflecting on God's faithfulness in the past help me to trust Him in the present and future?

_____
_____
_____
_____
_____
_____
_____
_____
_____
_____
_____
_____
_____

DAY 15

"Trust in the Lord with all your heart, and do not lean on your own understanding. In all your ways acknowledge him, and he will make straight your paths." (Proverbs 3:5-6, ESV) How can I surrender my own plans and desires to God during my devotionals, trusting that He will guide my steps?

_____

_____

_____

_____

_____

_____

_____

_____

_____

_____

_____

_____

_____

DAY 16

"**And let us not grow weary of doing good, for in due season we will reap, if we do not give up.**" **(Galatians 6:9, ESV)** How can my devotional time encourage me to persevere in faith, even when I don't see immediate results?

_____
_____
_____
_____
_____
_____
_____
_____
_____
_____
_____
_____

DAY 17

"Therefore, confess your sins to one another and pray for one another, that you may be healed. The prayer of a righteous person has great power as it is working." (James 5:16, ESV) How can I use my devotional time to confess my sins and seek forgiveness, allowing God to heal and restore me?

_____
_____
_____
_____
_____
_____
_____
_____
_____
_____
_____
_____

DAY 18

"But they who wait for the Lord shall renew their strength; they shall mount up with wings like eagles; they shall run and not be weary; they shall walk and not faint." (Isaiah 40:31, ESV) How can I wait on the Lord during my devotional time, allowing Him to renew my strength and restore my hope?

_____

_____

_____

_____

_____

_____

_____

_____

_____

_____

_____

_____

DAY 19

"The Lord is my rock and my fortress and my deliverer, my God, my rock, in whom I take refuge, my shield, and the horn of my salvation, my stronghold." (Psalm 18:2, ESV) How can I find refuge in God's presence during my devotional time, especially when I'm feeling overwhelmed or afraid?

DAY 20

"For God gave us a spirit not of fear but of power and love and self-control." (2 Timothy 1:7, ESV) How can I replace my fears and doubts with God's power, love, and self-control through prayer and reflection?

_____
_____
_____
_____
_____
_____
_____
_____
_____
_____
_____
_____
_____

DAY 21

"So faith comes from hearing, and hearing through the word of Christ." (Romans 10:17, ESV) How can I actively listen for God's voice during my devotional time, allowing His Word to speak to my heart and strengthen my faith?

_____

_____

_____

_____

_____

_____

_____

_____

_____

_____

_____

_____

_____

DAY 22

"The sacrifices of God are a broken spirit; a broken and contrite heart, O God, you will not despise." (Psalm 51:17, ESV) How can I approach God with a humble and contrite heart during my devotionals, acknowledging my need for His grace and forgiveness?

DAY 23

"Draw near to God, and he will draw near to you." (James 4:8a, ESV) How can I create space in my daily life for intentional connection with God, fostering a deeper and more intimate relationship with Him?

_____

_____

_____

_____

_____

_____

_____

_____

_____

_____

_____

_____

_____

_____

DAY 24

"And we know that for those who love God all things work together for good, for those who are called according to his purpose." (Romans 8:28, ESV) How can reflecting on this verse during my devotionals help me to trust in God's plan for my life, even when I face challenges or setbacks?

_____

_____

_____

_____

_____

_____

_____

_____

_____

_____

_____

_____

DAY 25

"Delight yourself in the Lord, and he will give you the desires of your heart." (Psalm 37:4, ESV) How can I cultivate a deeper delight in God through my devotional practices, allowing Him to shape my desires and align them with His will?

_____
_____
_____
_____
_____
_____
_____
_____
_____
_____
_____
_____
_____

DAY 26

"Do not be anxious about tomorrow, for tomorrow will be anxious for itself. Sufficient for the day is its own trouble." (Matthew 6:34, ESV) How can I focus on trusting God in the present moment, rather than worrying about the future, during my devotionals?

_____

_____

_____

_____

_____

_____

_____

_____

_____

_____

_____

_____

DAY 27

"I lift up my eyes to the hills. From where does my help come? My help comes from the Lord, who made heaven and earth." (Psalm 121:1-2, ESV) How can I look to God as my source of help and strength during my devotional time, especially when facinjog challenges or uncertainties?

DAY 28

"The Lord is my light and my salvation; whom shall I fear? The Lord is the stronghold of my life; of whom shall I be afraid?" (Psalm 27:1, ESV) How can I meditate on God's protection and provision during my devotionals, allowing His peace to dispel my fears and doubts?

_____
_____
_____
_____
_____
_____
_____
_____
_____
_____
_____
_____

DAY 29

"Create in me a clean heart, O God, and renew a right spirit within me." (Psalm 51:10, ESV) How can I use my devotional time to invite God to cleanse my heart and renew my spirit, creating a space for deeper trust and surrender?

_____
_____
_____
_____
_____
_____
_____
_____
_____
_____
_____
_____
_____

DAY 30

"**For we do not have a high priest who is unable to sympathize with our weaknesses, but one who in every respect has been tempted as we are, yet without sin. Let us then with confidence draw near to the throne of grace, that we may receive mercy and find grace to help in time of need.**" (Hebrews 4:15-16, ESV) How can I approach God's throne of grace with confidence during my devotional time, knowing that He understands my struggles and offers me mercy and grace?

Incorporating worship into daily routine

Music, with its ability to stir the soul and evoke deep emotions, holds a special place in the realm of worship. Whether it's the soaring melodies of a hymn, the rhythmic beats of a contemporary praise song, or the gentle strumming of a guitar, music has the power to transport us beyond the confines of our daily lives and into the presence of God. As we sing along, our hearts resonate with the lyrics, expressing our love, our gratitude, and our unwavering trust in Him.

Incorporating worship songs into your daily routine can be a transformative practice. Create a playlist of songs that speak to your heart and uplift your spirit. Listen to them as you commute to work, exercise, or simply relax at home. Allow the melodies and lyrics to wash over you, reminding you of God's goodness, His faithfulness, and His promises for your life.

As you engage with the music, pay attention to the words. What truths about God are being expressed? What emotions are being evoked? How do these songs resonate with your own experiences of faith and doubt? Allow the music to become a soundtrack for your spiritual journey, a constant reminder of God's presence and His unwavering love.

But worship is not just about listening to music; it's also about actively engaging with God through prayer. As you sing along to your favourite worship songs, allow your heart to overflow with prayerful expressions of gratitude, adoration, and surrender. Thank God for His blessings, both big and small. Praise Him for His character, His power, and His unfailing love. And bring your doubts and uncertainties before Him, trusting that He hears your every word and longs to meet you in your vulnerability.

This practice of prayerful worship can transform even the most mundane moments into sacred encounters with God. As you fold laundry, wash dishes, or commute to work, you can offer up prayers of thanksgiving, intercession, and surrender. You can turn your heart towards Him, acknowledging His presence in every aspect of your life.

Creating a dedicated space for worship in your home can also be a powerful way to cultivate a deeper connection with God. This space doesn't have to be elaborate or extravagant; it can be a simple corner of your bedroom, a quiet spot in your living room, or even a comfortable chair on your porch. The key is to create an environment that invites you to focus on God, to set aside distractions, and to engage in intentional acts of worship.

You might consider adding elements to your worship space that inspire and uplift you. These could include candles, artwork, inspirational quotes, or even natural elements like flowers or plants. You might also create a playlist of worship music that you can listen to in this space, allowing the melodies and lyrics to fill your heart and mind with God's truth.

This dedicated space can become a sanctuary, a place where you can retreat from the busyness of life and connect with God on a deeper level. It can also be a place where you gather with family or friends for prayer, worship, and fellowship, strengthening your faith through shared experiences.

In addition to personal worship, participating in community worship events can also be a powerful way to build faith and overcome doubt. When we gather with other believers to sing praises, offer prayers, and hear God's Word proclaimed, we experience a sense of belonging and connection that transcends our individual struggles. We are reminded that we are part of a larger body, a community of faith that supports and encourages one another on the journey.

Community worship also provides opportunities to encounter diverse expressions of faith. We hear the voices of others lifted in song, their unique perspectives and experiences adding depth and richness to our own understanding of God. We witness the power of collective prayer, as individual petitions merge into a chorus of supplication and praise. And we are reminded that we are not alone in our doubts and uncertainties, that countless others are wrestling with similar questions and seeking to deepen their trust in God.

In the shared experience of community worship, we find strength, encouragement, and a renewed sense of hope. We are reminded that God is at work in the world, moving in the hearts of His people and drawing us closer to Himself. We are invited to participate in His story, to offer our own voices in praise and adoration, and to trust that He is leading us towards a future filled with purpose and fulfillment.

Incorporating worship into your daily routine is not about adding another item to your to-do list; it's about transforming your everyday life into an ongoing act of devotion. It's about finding moments throughout your day to connect with God, to express your love for Him, and to seek His guidance and strength.

Whether it's through music, prayer, creating a worship space, or participating in community events, there are countless ways to infuse your life with worship. As you do so, you will find that your faith deepens, your trust in God grows stronger, and your doubts begin to fade. You will discover that worship is not just an activity; it's a way of life, a posture of the heart that invites God's presence into every aspect of your being.

Navigating Life Transitions with Faith

"Even though I walk through the valley of the shadow of death, I will fear no evil, for you are with me; your rod and your staff, they comfort me." (Psalm 23:4, ESV)

Life's journey is rarely a smooth path; it's often marked by twists and turns, uphill climbs, and unexpected detours. We encounter moments of joy and celebration, but also seasons of loss, change, and profound challenge. These transitions, whether anticipated or unforeseen, can shake the very foundations of our lives, leaving us feeling disoriented and uncertain. In the midst of these upheavals, our faith is often tested, and our trust in God may waver. Doubts may creep in, whispering questions about His goodness, His sovereignty, and His plans for our lives. We may find ourselves grappling with feelings of fear, anxiety, and even anger, as we struggle to reconcile our circumstances with our beliefs.

Yet, it is precisely in these moments of transition, when the familiar gives way to the unknown, that we have the opportunity to experience God's presence and guidance in a profound way. It's in the midst of change and uncertainty that we can lean into Him more deeply, seeking His wisdom, His comfort, and His strength to navigate the uncharted waters ahead.

This chapter focuses on the importance of trusting God during significant life changes and challenges, emphasizing that these transitions are opportunities to deepen our faith, even when doubt prevails. We'll explore how to navigate the turbulent waters of loss and grief, finding solace and strength in God's unwavering love. We'll explore the complexities of career changes, learning to discern God's guidance and to trust His provision even when the path forward seems unclear. And we'll examine the challenges of relational shifts, discovering how to maintain healthy connections and to rely on God's wisdom in navigating conflict and change.

Throughout this chapter, we'll draw inspiration from biblical figures who faced their own life transitions with courage and faith. We'll see how they wrestled with doubt, sought God's guidance, and ultimately emerged from their trials with a deeper trust in His promises. We'll also explore practical strategies for cultivating faith during times of change, including prayer, Scripture reading, and seeking support from the Christian community.

Remember, life transitions, while often challenging, are not meant to derail our faith. They are opportunities for growth, for transformation, and for a deeper reliance on God's grace. They are invitations to step out in faith, to embrace the unknown, and to trust that God is with us every step of the way.

Handling Loss and Grief with Faith

The pain of loss, whether through death, a broken relationship, or a shattered dream, can leave us feeling lost, alone, and questioning the very foundations of our faith. It's in these moments of profound sorrow that doubts may surface, whispering accusations against God's goodness and His plans for our lives. We may find ourselves asking, "Where is God in my pain?" or "Why has He allowed this to happen?"

Yet, even in the depths of our grief, we are not alone. The Bible assures us that God is near to the brokenhearted and saves the crushed in spirit. (Psalm 34:18, ESV) He is a God of compassion and comfort, who weeps with us in our sorrow and offers us His strength and solace.

"Blessed be the God and Father of our Lord Jesus Christ, the Father of mercies and God of all comfort, who comforts us in all our affliction, so that we may be able to comfort those who are in any affliction, with the comfort with which we ourselves are comforted by God." (2 Corinthians 1:3-4, ESV)

This passage reminds us that God is not a distant observer of our pain; He is intimately acquainted with our suffering and offers us His comfort in abundance. His presence, like a warm embrace, surrounds us in our grief, offering a sense of peace and hope that transcends our circumstances.

The process of mourning is a natural and necessary part of the human experience. It's a journey that takes time, patience, and a willingness to confront the full range of emotions that accompany loss. We may experience anger, sadness, guilt, or even numbness. We may struggle to sleep, to eat, or to find joy in the things that once brought us pleasure.

It's important to remember that these emotions are not signs of weakness or a lack of faith. They are a natural response to loss, a way of processing the pain and coming to terms with the reality of our changed circumstances. The Bible itself is filled with expressions of grief and lament, from the Psalms of David to the book of Lamentations. These texts remind us that it's okay to grieve, to express our sorrow and anger before God, and to seek His comfort in the midst of our pain.

As you grieve, also take time to celebrate the life of the one you've lost. Remember the good times, the shared laughter, and the precious memories that will forever be etched in your heart. Share stories with others, create a memorial, or engage in activities that honor the legacy of your loved one.

This act of remembrance can be a source of healing and hope. It allows you to cherish the time you had with your loved one, to acknowledge the impact they had on your life, and to find gratitude in the midst of sorrow. It also reminds you that death is not the end, that there is a hope of resurrection and eternal life through faith in Jesus Christ.

"For we know that if the tent that is our earthly home is destroyed, we have a building from God, a house not made with hands, eternal in the heavens." (2 Corinthians 5:1, ESV)

During times of grief, the support of your faith community can be invaluable. Surround yourself with people who will listen without judgment, offer words of comfort, and pray for you. Attend church services, participate in small groups, or seek out counseling from a pastor or spiritual leader.

The shared experience of grief can create a powerful bond within a community. As you gather with others who are also mourning, you can find strength in their presence, encouragement in their words, and hope in their shared faith. You can also offer your own support to others, reminding them that they are not alone and that God is with them in their pain.

Trusting God's Plan during Career Changes

When a layoff notice arrives, a dream job falls through, or a burning passion for a new field ignites within us? These moments of career transition, while often filled with both excitement and trepidation, can test the very foundations of our trust in God.

It's easy to fall into the trap of anxiety and doubt when faced with career changes. We may question God's plans, wonder if we're making the right choices, or grapple with the fear of financial insecurity. We may find ourselves clinging to the familiar, even when it no longer brings us joy or aligns with our deepest values. In these moments of uncertainty, it's essential to remember that God is not a passive observer of our lives; He is actively involved in every aspect of our journey, including our careers.

Seeking divine guidance is crucial as we navigate career transitions. Through prayer, we can invite God into our decision-making processes, seeking His wisdom and discernment. We can ask Him to reveal His will for our lives, to open doors of opportunity, and to close those that lead us astray. We can also express our fears and anxieties, trusting that He hears our every word and longs to comfort us in our distress.

One powerful way to seek God's guidance is through a practice known as **"Lectio Divina"** or divine reading. Choose a passage of Scripture that speaks to the themes of work, purpose, or provision. Read the passage slowly and prayerfully, meditating on its words and allowing them to sink deep into your heart. As you read, listen for God's voice, paying attention to any *insights*, impressions, or convictions that arise within you.

Another helpful practice is to create a **"career vision board."** Gather images, quotes, and scriptures that represent your aspirations and dreams for your professional life. As you create your board, pray for God's guidance and direction. Ask Him to reveal His plans for your career and to align your desires with His will.

While seeking God's guidance is essential, it's equally important to embrace change as an opportunity for growth. Just as a caterpillar must undergo a metamorphosis to become a butterfly, we too must be willing to embrace change in order to reach our full potential. Career transitions, while often challenging, can be catalysts for personal and spiritual development. They can push us outside our comfort zones, forcing us to rely on God's strength and provision in new and unexpected ways.

The Bible is filled with stories of individuals who experienced significant career changes and found their faith deepened in the process. Joseph, sold into slavery by his own brothers, endured years of hardship and injustice before ultimately rising to a position of power and influence in Egypt. His story reminds us that God can use even the most difficult circumstances to fulfill His purposes and to bring about His good.

Similarly, the apostle Paul, once a persecutor of Christians, experienced a dramatic conversion that led him to abandon his former life and dedicate himself to spreading the Gospel. His story demonstrates that God can radically redirect our paths, calling us to new and unexpected vocations that align with His will for our lives.

Of course, career changes often come with a host of emotions, including fear, anxiety, and uncertainty. It's natural to worry about the future, to question your abilities, or to feel overwhelmed by the unknown. But in these moments of emotional turmoil, we can find comfort and reassurance in God's promises.

"Do not be anxious about anything, but in every situation, by prayer and petition, with thanksgiving, present your requests to God. And the peace of God, which transcends all understanding, will guard your hearts and your minds in Christ Jesus." (Philippians 4:6-7, NIV).

This passage reminds us that we don't have to face our fears alone. We can bring them before God in prayer, trusting that He will hear us, comfort us, and give us the peace that surpasses all understanding. We can also turn to Scripture for encouragement, reminding ourselves of God's faithfulness throughout history and His promises to provide for our needs.

Maintaining Faith Through Illness

When the unwelcome specter of illness descends upon us, casting its shadow over our lives, it can feel as if the very foundations of our faith are shaken. Physical pain, emotional turmoil, and the uncertainty of the future can create a breeding ground for doubt and despair. We may find ourselves questioning God's goodness, His sovereignty, and His plans for our lives. We may wrestle with feelings of anger, fear, and even abandonment, as we grapple with the limitations and vulnerabilities of our human existence.

Illness, whether chronic or acute, can be a profound test of faith. It can disrupt our routines, shatter our dreams, and challenge our deepest beliefs about God and His purposes. We may find ourselves asking, "Why me?" or "Why now?" We may struggle to reconcile the reality of our suffering with the image of a loving and compassionate God.

It's important to acknowledge that these feelings are normal and natural. The Bible itself is filled with stories of individuals who wrestled with faith in the face of illness and hardship. From Job's agonizing lamentations to Paul's "thorn in the flesh," we see that even the most devout believers can experience moments of doubt and despair when confronted with physical or mental challenges.

But even in the midst of our pain and confusion, we are not alone. God is with us, offering His comfort, His strength, and His unwavering love. He is the Great Physician, the Healer of our souls and bodies. He is also the God of all comfort, who understands our deepest fears and anxieties and longs to bring us peace in the midst of the storm.

Prayer becomes a lifeline in times of illness, a channel through which we can pour out our hearts to God and seek His healing touch. It's a way of acknowledging our dependence on Him, surrendering our fears and anxieties to His care, and inviting Him to intervene in our circumstances.

"Do not be anxious about anything, but in every situation, by prayer and petition, with thanksgiving, present your requests to God. And the peace of God, which transcends all understanding, will guard your hearts and your minds in Christ Jesus." (Philippians 4:6-7, NIV)

This passage reminds us that prayer is not just about asking for healing; it's also about finding peace in God's presence, even when healing may not come in the way we expect. It's about surrendering our will to His, trusting that He knows what is best for us, even in the midst of suffering.

Throughout history, countless individuals have found strength and solace in prayer during times of illness. From the early church fathers to modern-day saints, their stories testify to the transformative power of prayer in the face of adversity. They remind us that even when our bodies are weak, our spirits can be strong, anchored in the hope of God's promises.

While prayer is a vital part of navigating illness with faith, it's also important to remember that God's healing can take many forms. It may be physical, emotional, or spiritual. It may come instantly, or it may unfold gradually over time. And sometimes, healing may not come in this life, but rather in the promise of eternal life with Christ.

It's important to avoid the trap of believing that if we just pray hard enough, God is obligated to heal us. While He is certainly capable of miraculous intervention, He also works through the natural processes of medicine and science. Our faith does not negate the need for medical treatment or the reality of our physical limitations.

Instead, we can view illness as an opportunity to deepen our relationship with God, to seek His wisdom and guidance, and to discover new depths of His love and grace. We can trust that He is with us in our suffering, that He understands our pain, and that He will use even the most difficult circumstances for our good and His glory.

In the words of the apostle Paul, ***"And we know that in all things God works for the good of those who love him, who have been called according to his purpose." (Romans 8:28, NIV)***

As you navigate the challenges of illness, remember that you are not alone. God is with you, offering His comfort, His strength, and His unwavering love. Lean into Him, seek His guidance, and trust in His promises. And remember, even in the midst of suffering, you can find hope, purpose, and a deeper connection with the One who holds your future in His hands.

Overcoming External Skepticism and Influences

"Do not be surprised, brothers, that the world hates you." (1 John 3:13, ESV).

In a world that often views faith with skepticism, cynicism, or even outright hostility, maintaining a steadfast trust in God can be a formidable challenge. The voices of doubt and disbelief, amplified by the megaphone of popular culture and social media, can chip away at our convictions, leaving us feeling isolated, defensive, and questioning the very foundations of our faith. We may encounter friends, family members, or colleagues who challenge our beliefs, presenting arguments that seem logical and compelling. We may be bombarded with news stories that portray religion in a negative light, highlighting hypocrisy, scandals, or the perceived conflict between faith and science. And we may even experience subtle or overt discrimination for our beliefs, feeling pressured to conform to a secular worldview or to keep our faith private and hidden.

These external forces, if left unchecked, can plant seeds of doubt in our hearts, eroding our confidence and undermining our trust in God. We may find ourselves questioning the validity of our beliefs, wondering if we're simply naive or delusional for holding onto something that others find so easily dismissed. We may feel a sense of shame or embarrassment, as if our faith is a mark of intellectual inferiority or social backwardness.

However, as believers, we are called to stand firm in our faith, even in the face of opposition and ridicule. We are reminded in 1 Peter 3:15, **"But in your hearts honor Christ the Lord as holy, always being prepared to make a defense to anyone who asks you for a reason for the hope that is in you; yet do it with gentleness and respect."** This verse encourages us to be ready to articulate our beliefs, to share the reasons for our hope, and to do so with grace and humility.

Engaging in respectful dialogue with those who hold differing viewpoints can be a powerful way to strengthen our own convictions and to witness to the transformative power of faith. It's an opportunity to demonstrate that faith is not blind adherence to dogma, but a reasoned and thoughtful response to the complexities of life and the human condition. It's also a chance to build bridges of understanding, to foster mutual respect, and to demonstrate the love and compassion that lie at the heart of the Christian faith.

Of course, not all conversations about faith will be productive or fruitful. There may be times when we encounter individuals who are closed-minded or hostile, who are more interested in winning an argument than in seeking truth. In these situations, it's important to exercise discernment and to know when to walk away. We are not obligated to engage in every debate or to defend our faith against every attack. Sometimes, the most powerful witness we can offer is a life lived in accordance with God's truth, a life that radiates love, joy, and peace, even in the face of adversity.

In addition to engaging in dialogue, it's also important to cultivate a strong foundation of personal conviction. This involves delving deeper into Scripture, studying the teachings of the Church, and seeking wisdom from trusted mentors and spiritual leaders. The more we understand the reasons for our faith, the more equipped we will be to withstand the challenges and criticisms of the world.

It's also helpful to surround ourselves with a supportive community of believers who can offer encouragement and accountability. In the company of others who share our faith, we find strength, solidarity, and a reminder that we are not alone in our journey. We can share our struggles openly, knowing that we will be met with understanding and support. We can also learn from the experiences of others, gaining wisdom and insights that can help us navigate the complexities of faith in a skeptical world.

Ultimately, overcoming external skepticism and influences requires a combination of courage, conviction, and grace. It's about standing firm in our faith, even when it's unpopular or inconvenient. It's about being ready to articulate our beliefs with gentleness and respect. And it's about surrounding ourselves with a supportive community that will encourage us, challenge us, and remind us of the truth that sets us free.

As you navigate the challenges of living out your faith in a skeptical world, remember that you are not alone. God is with you, strengthening you, and empowering you to be a light in the darkness. Trust in His promises, lean on His strength, and let your life be a testament to the transformative power of His love.

Understanding Emotional Triggers

One of the ways of Overcoming External Skepticism and Influences, as earlier mentioned, is managing criticism from non-believers. In a world where faith is often met with indifference, skepticism, or even hostility, encountering criticism from those who do not share our beliefs is an inevitable part of the Christian journey. These encounters, while potentially unsettling, can also be opportunities for growth, for deepening our convictions, and for demonstrating the love and grace that lie at the heart of our faith.

Understanding the nature of criticism is a crucial first step in navigating these encounters. It's important to recognize that criticism often stems from misunderstanding or a lack of exposure to genuine faith. Non-believers may have encountered negative portrayals of Christianity in the media or may have had personal experiences that have left them feeling hurt or disillusioned by religion. Their criticisms, while sometimes harsh or insensitive, may reflect their own struggles and uncertainties rather than a personal attack on you or your beliefs.

By approaching criticism with empathy and understanding, we can disarm its sting and create opportunities for meaningful dialogue. We can acknowledge the validity of their concerns, share our own experiences of faith, and invite them to consider a different perspective. We can also demonstrate the transformative power of faith in our own lives, showing them that Christianity is not just a set of rules or doctrines, but a living relationship with a loving God.

Preparing thoughtful responses to criticism is another essential tool for navigating these encounters. When we are able to articulate our beliefs clearly and confidently, we not only strengthen our own convictions but also demonstrate to others that faith is not blind adherence to dogma, but a reasoned and thoughtful response to the complexities of life and the human condition.

Take time to reflect on the common criticisms you encounter and to develop responses that are grounded in Scripture, personal experience, and sound reasoning. Practice these responses with trusted friends or family members, refining your language and ensuring that your message is clear and compelling. Remember, you don't have to have all the answers; it's okay to acknowledge that some questions remain unanswered or that certain aspects of faith are beyond human comprehension.

While engaging in dialogue with non-believers can be fruitful, it's also important to recognize that not all conversations are created equal. There may be times when you encounter individuals who are closed-minded or hostile, who are more interested in winning an argument than in seeking truth. In these situations, it's important to set boundaries and to know when to disengage.

You are not obligated to defend your faith against every attack or to engage in every debate. Sometimes, the most powerful witness you can offer is a life lived in accordance with God's truth, a life that radiates love, joy, and peace, even in the face of adversity. By gracefully withdrawing from unproductive conversations, you protect your own mental and spiritual well-being and create space for more meaningful encounters in the future.

In the midst of criticism and opposition, it's crucial to seek support from your fellow believers. Surround yourself with people who will uplift and encourage you, who will remind you of God's truth, and who will pray for you as you navigate these challenges. Share your experiences with trusted friends or mentors, allowing them to offer their own insights and perspectives.

Remember, the Christian community is a source of strength and solidarity(I can't overemphasize this enough).It is a place where you can find refuge in times of doubt and uncertainty. By leaning on the support of your fellow believers, you can weather the storms of criticism and emerge with a stronger, more resilient faith.

Ultimately, managing criticism from non-believers is not about winning arguments or proving your point. It's about living out your faith with integrity, grace, and compassion. It's about being prepared to share the reasons for your hope, while also respecting the beliefs of others. And it's about trusting that God is with you, strengthening you, and empowering you to be a faithful witness in a world that desperately needs His love.

Strengthening Internal Convictions

Another way of Overcoming External Skepticism and Influences, as earlier mentioned, is by strengthening internal convictions. While engaging with external skepticism is undoubtedly important, it's equally crucial to fortify the internal foundations of our faith. When our beliefs are rooted in a deep understanding of God's Word and a personal experience of His love, we are better equipped to withstand the winds of doubt and criticism that may blow against us.

"But the one who looks into the perfect law, the law of liberty, and perseveres, being no hearer who forgets but a doer who acts, he will be blessed in his doing." (James 1:25, ESV). This verse speaks to the transformative power of engaging with Scripture, not just as passive observers, but as active participants. When we delve into the Bible with a heart seeking understanding and a willingness to apply its teachings to our lives, we cultivate a faith that is both intellectually sound and personally meaningful.

Setting aside dedicated time for personal reflection on your faith is a crucial step in strengthening your convictions. Carve out moments in your day to ponder the core tenets of your beliefs, to examine the reasons for your hope, and to consider how your faith shapes your worldview and your interactions with others. Journaling can be a helpful tool for this process, allowing you to articulate your thoughts and feelings, to track your spiritual growth, and to identify areas where you may need further exploration or clarification.

Regular engagement with Scripture is another vital practice for strengthening your internal convictions. The Bible, as the inspired Word of God, offers a wealth of wisdom, guidance, and reassurance for those who seek to deepen their faith. As you read and study its pages, you encounter stories of individuals who wrestled with their own doubts and fears, yet ultimately found solace and strength in God's unwavering love and faithfulness.

You also encounter the very words of God, spoken through prophets, poets, and apostles, revealing His character, His promises, and His plans for your lives. These words, when internalized and applied, have the power to transform your heart and mind, shaping your beliefs, your attitudes, and your actions.

Consider memorizing key verses that speak to your specific struggles or that offer particular encouragement and reassurance. These verses, etched into your memory, can become a source of strength and comfort in moments of doubt or temptation. They can also serve as a powerful tool for sharing your faith with others, providing a clear and concise articulation of your beliefs.

Seeking out spiritual mentors can also be invaluable in strengthening your convictions. These mentors, whether pastors, teachers, or simply mature believers who have walked the path of faith before you, can offer guidance, wisdom, and encouragement as you navigate your own journey. They can help you to understand complex theological concepts, to wrestle with difficult questions, and to find clarity and direction in the midst of uncertainty.

Mentors can also provide a safe space for you to share your doubts and fears without judgment or condemnation. They can listen with empathy and understanding, offer insights from their own experiences, and point you towards resources that can further deepen your faith. Their presence in your life can be a source of immense strength and encouragement, reminding you that you are not alone and that God is faithful to meet us in our moments of need.

Finally, establishing regular spiritual practices can be a powerful way to reinforce your trust in God and to cultivate a deeper connection with Him. These practices might include prayer, meditation, fasting, or engaging in acts of service and compassion. By incorporating these disciplines into your daily routine, you create a rhythm of faith that sustains you through the ups and downs of life.

As you engage in these practices, pay attention to the ways in which they impact your heart, your mind, and your relationship with God. Do you find yourself experiencing a greater sense of peace and joy? Are you developing a deeper understanding of His Word and His will for your life? Are you becoming more compassionate and generous towards others?

These spiritual practices, when cultivated with intentionality and consistency, can have a profound impact on your faith journey. They can help you to internalize God's truth, to develop a deeper trust in His promises, and to stand firm in your convictions, even in the face of external skepticism and doubt.

Remember, strengthening your internal convictions is not a one-time event; it's an ongoing process that requires commitment and perseverance. But as you invest in your relationship with God, as you seek His wisdom and guidance, and as you allow His love to transform your heart, you will find that your faith becomes a beacon of light, shining brightly in a world shrouded in darkness.

Living a Balanced Life

"For in this hope we were saved. Now hope that is seen is not hope. For who hopes for what he sees? But if we hope for what we do not see, we wait for it with patience." (Romans 8:24-25, ESV)

In the swirling mists of uncertainty, where the path ahead is obscured and the future seems veiled in shadows, hope emerges as a beacon of light, guiding us through the darkness and anchoring our souls in the midst of life's storms. It's a tenacious flame that flickers even in the face of doubt, a quiet whisper that reminds us of God's promises and His unwavering love.

Hope, in the Christian context, is not merely a wishful longing or a naive optimism. It's a confident expectation, a firm belief that God is at work, even when we can't see the evidence of His hand. It's a steadfast trust in His goodness, His sovereignty, and His ultimate plan for our lives, even when circumstances seem bleak or uncertain.

This chapter explores the transformative power of hope, especially when faced with the challenges of skepticism and uncertainty. We will examine the ways in which hope can anchor us in times of doubt, providing a sense of peace and purpose amidst the chaos of life. We will explore practical strategies for cultivating hope in our daily lives, allowing it to permeate our thoughts, our actions, and our relationships.

Hope is not a passive emotion; it's an active choice, a decision to trust in God's goodness and His faithfulness, even when we can't see the way forward. It's a refusal to succumb to despair or to allow fear to dictate our lives. It's a bold declaration that we believe in a God who is bigger than our circumstances, who holds the future in His hands, and who is working all things together for our good.

As we cultivate hope in our lives, we discover a wellspring of strength and resilience that sustains us through life's challenges. We find the courage to face the unknown, the perseverance to endure through trials, and the peace that transcends our circumstances. We also become beacons of light to those around us, offering hope and encouragement to those who are struggling to find their way.

May this chapter inspire you to embrace uncertainty with hope, to trust in God's guidance, and discover the transformative power of faith in the midst of life's storms.

Biblical foundations for hope

Paul's letter to the Hebrews, addressing a community grappling with persecution and hardship, offers a powerful metaphor for hope: ***"We have this as a sure and steadfast anchor of the soul, a hope that enters into the inner place behind the curtain, where Jesus has gone as*** *a forerunner on our behalf, having become a high priest forever after the order of Melchizedek." (Hebrews 6:19-20, ESV)*

Hope, in this context, is likened to an anchor, providing stability and security amidst the turbulent seas of life. It's a steadfast assurance that even when the waves crash and the winds howl, we are tethered to something greater than ourselves, something that cannot be shaken or moved. This anchor is not merely a symbol of wishful thinking; it's rooted in the very character of God, His unchanging nature, and His unwavering commitment to His people.

When doubts arise, when the future seems uncertain, we can cling to this anchor of hope, reminding ourselves that God's promises are true and that His love endures forever. We can trust that even in the midst of our struggles, He is working behind the scenes, orchestrating events for our good and His glory. We can rest in the assurance that He will never leave us or forsake us, that He is with us always, even to the end of the age.

The prophet Jeremiah, speaking to a nation in exile, offers another powerful reminder of God's faithfulness and His plans for our lives. *"For I know the plans I have for you, declares the Lord, plans for welfare and not for evil, to give you a future and a hope." (Jeremiah 29:11, ESV)* This verse, often quoted in times of transition or uncertainty, speaks to the heart of our longing for reassurance. It reminds us that God has a purpose for our lives, a plan that is good and filled with hope.

Even when we can't see the road ahead, we can trust that He is leading us towards a future that is far greater than anything we could imagine. This knowledge can anchor us in times of doubt, reminding us that our lives are not random or meaningless. We are part of a larger story, a divine narrative that is unfolding according to God's perfect will.

While the Old Testament lays the foundation for hope, it is in the New Testament that we find its ultimate fulfillment. Jesus Christ, the Son of God, embodies and provides the hope that we so desperately need. His resurrection from the dead, the cornerstone of Christian faith, is a triumphant declaration that death has been defeated, and that eternal life is available to all who believe in Him.

"May the God of hope fill you with all joy and peace in believing, so that by the power of the Holy Spirit you may abound in hope." (Romans 15:13, ESV). This verse, addressed to the early Christians in Rome, reminds us that hope is not just a fleeting emotion; it's a gift from God, poured into our hearts through the Holy Spirit. It's a source of joy and peace, even in the midst of trials and tribulations.

As we encounter challenges and uncertainties in our lives, we can turn to Jesus, the author and perfecter of our faith, for hope and encouragement. His life, marked by compassion, sacrifice, and unwavering trust in His Father, serves as a model for us to follow. His resurrection, the ultimate victory over sin and death, assures us that even in the darkest of times, there is always hope.

Personal stories of overcoming uncertainty

Let me share with you a personal experience that shook the very foundations of my trust in God. It was a time of profound loss and grief, a season when the familiar comforts of my life seemed to crumble beneath my feet. The weight of sorrow pressed heavily upon me, and doubts whispered insidious questions in my ears: "Where is God in this pain? Has He abandoned me? Will I ever find joy again?"

In those darkest hours, I clung to the lifeline of prayer, pouring out my heart to God with raw honesty and vulnerability. I questioned, I cried, I even raged against the injustice of it all. But through it all, I held onto a flicker of hope, a faint whisper in my soul that reminded me of God's promises and His unwavering love.

As the days turned into weeks and the weeks into months, I began to notice subtle shifts in my perspective. The fog of grief began to lift, and I saw glimpses of God's grace shining through the cracks of my broken heart. I found comfort in the embrace of my faith community, in the shared tears and prayers of those who loved me. And I discovered a newfound strength in the pages of Scripture, where the stories of those who had walked through their own valleys of sorrow offered me hope and encouragement.

One day, as I was reading the Psalms, a particular verse jumped off the page: "The Lord is close to the brokenhearted and saves those who are crushed in spirit." (Psalm 34:18, ESV) In that moment, I felt a profound sense of God's presence, a reassurance that He was with me in my pain, holding me close and offering me His comfort. It was as if a weight had been lifted from my shoulders, and a glimmer of hope began to flicker within my heart.

As I continued to seek God's presence through prayer, Scripture reading, and fellowship with other believers, I began to see how He was using this season of grief to refine my faith and deepen my trust in Him. I learned to rely on His strength rather than my own, to surrender my anxieties to His care, and to find peace in His promises, even when my circumstances remained uncertain.

My journey through grief was not a linear one. There were setbacks and moments of discouragement, times when doubt threatened to overwhelm me once again. But through it all, I held onto the hope that God was with me, that He had a purpose for my pain, and that He would ultimately bring beauty from ashes.

And He did. In the months and years that followed, I witnessed His faithfulness in countless ways. He provided for my needs, He surrounded me with loving and supportive friends, and He gave me a renewed sense of purpose and direction. I emerged from the valley of grief with a deeper faith, a more profound understanding of His love, and an unwavering trust in His promises.

My story is not unique. Countless individuals within the Christian community have experienced their own journeys of doubt and uncertainty, followed by a renewed sense of hope and trust in God.

One friend shared how a devastating health diagnosis had shattered her world, leaving her feeling angry and betrayed. But through prayer, Scripture reading, and the support of her church family, she found a way to reconcile her pain with her faith. She discovered a deeper intimacy with God in the midst of her suffering, and she emerged from her ordeal with a renewed sense of purpose and a passion for helping others who were facing similar challenges.

Another friend recounted how a job loss had triggered a crisis of faith, leaving him questioning God's provision and His plans for his life. But as he sought God's guidance and leaned on the support of his community, he discovered new opportunities and a renewed sense of calling. He realized that God had been preparing him for a different path, one that aligned more closely with his gifts and passions.

These stories, and countless others like them, remind us that we are not alone in our struggles. They offer hope and encouragement, demonstrating that even in the midst of uncertainty, God is at work, weaving a tapestry of redemption and restoration. They also invite us to share our own stories, to create spaces within our communities where vulnerability is honored and authenticity is celebrated.

Living out hope in daily actions

Hope, like a radiant sunrise after a long night, has the power to pierce through the clouds of uncertainty and illuminate the path ahead. It is not a passive sentiment, but an active force that can be cultivated and expressed through our daily actions, even in the face of skepticism and doubt. When we choose to live out hope, we become conduits of God's light, radiating His love and grace to a world in need.

Another of the most potent ways to cultivate hope is through acts of kindness. When we extend a helping hand to those in need, offer a listening ear to a burdened heart, or simply share a smile with a stranger, we plant seeds of hope that can blossom into something beautiful. These seemingly small gestures, rooted in compassion and empathy, can have a ripple effect, touching the lives of others and reminding them that they are not alone.

But acts of kindness not only impact those who receive them; they also have a transformative effect on the giver. As we step outside ourselves and focus on the needs of others, we shift our perspective from our own problems to the larger tapestry of human experience. We discover a sense of purpose and meaning that transcends our own circumstances, and we tap into a wellspring of joy that flows from serving others in love.

Consider the simple act of paying for the coffee of the person behind you in line. It's a small gesture, but it can brighten someone's day and create a sense of connection and generosity. Or imagine volunteering at a local soup kitchen or homeless shelter, offering your time and skills to those who are struggling. These acts of service, while not always glamorous or easy, can be deeply fulfilling, reminding us of the interconnectedness of humanity and the power of compassion to bring about change.

Creating a hope-filled environment is yet another powerful way to cultivate a spirit of optimism and resilience. Whether it's in your home, your workplace, or your social circles, you can intentionally foster an atmosphere that promotes positivity, encouragement, and support.

Start by engaging in uplifting conversations. Instead of dwelling on negativity or complaining about your circumstances, choose to focus on the good things in your life and the blessings that God has bestowed upon you. Share stories of hope and resilience, celebrate the victories of others, and offer words of encouragement to those who are struggling.

You can also create a physical environment that reflects hope and positivity. Decorate your home or workspace with inspiring artwork, uplifting quotes, or images that remind you of God's promises. Surround yourself with books, music, and media that uplift your spirit and reinforce your faith. And make a conscious effort to limit your exposure to negativity and cynicism, choosing instead to focus on the good, the true, and the beautiful.

In addition to creating a hope-filled environment, consider incorporating daily practices into your routine that reinforce your trust in God and cultivate a spirit of optimism. These practices might include gratitude journaling, where you take time each day to write down the things you're thankful for, or positive affirmations, where you speak words of truth and encouragement over yourself.

Moving Forward with Renewed Faith

Having journeyed together through the valleys of doubt, explored the depths of personal struggles, sought divine reassurance, and learned from the timeless wisdom of biblical figures, we now turn to the concluding chapter of this transformative exploration. The path we've walked has not been easy; it has been marked by questions, uncertainties, and moments of profound wrestling with faith. Yet, through it all, we have discovered the enduring power of God's love, the steadfastness of His promises, and the transformative potential of embracing His guidance amidst skepticism and uncertainty.

In this final chapter, we shift our focus from the present struggles to the future challenges that lie ahead. Life, with its unpredictable twists and turns, will inevitably present us with new opportunities for doubt and uncertainty. We may face unexpected setbacks, encounter unforeseen obstacles, or grapple with decisions that seem impossible to navigate. In these moments, it's easy to succumb to fear, anxiety, and a sense of hopelessness.

But as believers, we are not called to live in a state of perpetual apprehension. We are called to walk in faith, trusting that God is with us, that He holds the future in His hands, and that He is working all things together for our good. This chapter will equip you with the tools and strategies you need to face the future with confidence, grounded in a deep and abiding trust in God's love and faithfulness.

We will explore the importance of cultivating a proactive faith, one that anticipates challenges and prepares for them with wisdom and discernment. We will delve into the power of prayer, Scripture, and community support in building a strong foundation of trust that can withstand the storms of doubt and uncertainty.

As we embark on this final leg of our journey, let us remember that faith is not about eliminating all uncertainty; it's about embracing the unknown with a sense of hope and confidence in God's guidance. It's about recognizing that even in the midst of challenges, He is present, He is working, and He is leading us towards a future filled with purpose and fulfillment.

In the words of the apostle Paul, ***"I can do all things through Christ who strengthens me." (Philippians 4:13, ESV)***. May this chapter empower you to face the future with unwavering faith, knowing that with God, all things are possible.

Setting Future Faith Goals

As we embark on the final stretch of our journey, let's turn our gaze towards the horizon, where the future unfolds with its promises and uncertainties. Having traversed the valleys of doubt, wrestled with personal struggles, and sought solace in God's Word and community, we now stand equipped to face the challenges that lie ahead with a renewed sense of faith and a steadfast trust in God's guidance. But how do we maintain this momentum, ensuring that our trust remains strong even when the storms of life threaten to shake us? The answer lies in the intentional practice of setting future faith goals, charting a course that will guide us towards spiritual growth, maturity, and an unwavering reliance on God's unwavering love.

Setting faith goals is not merely a matter of creating a to-do list for our spiritual lives. It's about fostering an intentional and purposeful relationship with God, one that is marked by growth, transformation, and an ever-deepening trust in His plans. These goals should be rooted in our desire to know Him more intimately, to serve Him more faithfully, and to reflect His character more fully in our daily lives.

When our faith goals are clearly defined and articulated, they serve as anchors in the midst of life's storms. They remind us of our commitment to God, even when doubts and uncertainties arise. They provide a sense of direction and purpose, guiding our steps and shaping our decisions. And they offer a tangible measure of progress, allowing us to celebrate our victories and learn from our setbacks.

When you start setting your own faith goals, consider both short-term and long-term objectives. Short-term goals, such as committing to daily prayer or Scripture reading, can help you establish healthy spiritual habits and maintain momentum in your faith journey. Long-term goals, such as serving in a specific ministry or deepening your understanding of a particular theological concept, can provide a broader vision for your spiritual maturity and discipleship.

Both types of goals should be **SMART**: **S**pecific, **M**easurable, **A**chievable, **R**elevant, and **T**ime-bound. Instead of simply stating, "I want to read the Bible more," consider setting a goal like, "I will read one chapter of the Bible every morning before work for the next month." This specific and measurable goal provides clarity and accountability, making it easier to track your progress and stay motivated.

Accountability plays a crucial role in achieving our faith goals. Sharing your goals with a trusted friend, mentor, or spiritual leader can provide encouragement, support, and gentle reminders when you need them most. It also creates a sense of shared responsibility, as you both strive to grow in your faith and encourage one another along the way.

Regular check-ins with your accountability partner can be a valuable opportunity to discuss your progress, share your struggles, and celebrate your victories. These conversations can also provide a forum for deeper spiritual discussions, as you delve into Scripture together, explore theological concepts, and apply God's truth to your daily lives.

Remember, accountability is not about judgment or condemnation; it's about mutual support and encouragement. It's about creating a safe and loving space where you can be honest about your struggles and receive the grace and guidance you need to continue on your faith journey.

Regularly reviewing and reflecting on your goals can help you stay aligned with God's will and make necessary adjustments as your circumstances change. Ask yourself questions like:

- Are my goals still relevant to my current season of life?
- Am I making progress towards achieving them?
- Are there any obstacles or challenges that are hindering my growth?
- What new opportunities has God placed before me?

By remaining open to His guidance and willing to adjust your course as needed, you demonstrate a willingness to surrender your own agenda to His perfect will.

Creating a Spiritual Growth Plan

Setting future faith goals is not just about achieving personal milestones or checking items off a list. It's about cultivating a deeper relationship with God, one that is marked by trust, surrender, and a willingness to grow. It's about embracing the journey of faith, with all its twists and turns, knowing that God is with you every step of the way.

The journey of faith is a lifelong adventure, a continuous unfolding of God's grace and truth in our lives. While we've explored the complexities of doubt, the power of prayer, the solace found in community, and the importance of embracing uncertainty with hope, the road ahead calls for continued growth and a deepening trust in God. To navigate this path with purpose and intentionality, we need a roadmap – a spiritual growth plan that guides us towards a more vibrant and resilient faith.

Just as a skilled architect carefully assesses the landscape before designing a building, we too must take stock of our spiritual terrain. Where are the areas of strength in your faith? Where do you feel most grounded and secure in your relationship with God? Conversely, where are the areas of weakness, the places where doubt and uncertainty still linger? What aspects of your faith do you long to understand more deeply or to experience more fully?

This honest self-assessment is not an exercise in self-criticism; it's an invitation to embrace vulnerability and to acknowledge the areas where you need to grow. It's a recognition that faith is not a static state but a dynamic process, one that requires ongoing attention and cultivation. By identifying your areas of weakness, you create a roadmap for targeted spiritual development, allowing you to focus your efforts on the practices and disciplines that will most effectively strengthen your faith.

Once you've identified your growth areas, it's time to explore the vast array of resources available to support your journey. The Bible, of course, remains the cornerstone of our faith, offering timeless wisdom, guidance, and reassurance. As you delve into its pages, pay particular attention to the passages that speak to your specific struggles and questions.

Consider joining a Bible study group or seeking out a trusted mentor who can help you to understand the deeper meaning and application of Scripture. There are also countless books, podcasts, and online resources that offer insights into various aspects of faith and can provide encouragement and support as you navigate your own journey.

In addition to intellectual engagement with the Bible and other resources, it's important to incorporate practical routines into your daily life that foster spiritual growth. These routines, like the steady rhythm of a heartbeat, create a sense of consistency and commitment to your faith journey. They provide opportunities for regular connection with God, for reflection on His Word, and for the cultivation of a deeper trust in His promises.

Consider setting aside time each day for prayer, Scripture reading, and meditation. These practices, when woven into the fabric of your daily life, can have a profound impact on your spiritual well-being. They create space for you to encounter God's presence, to listen for His voice, and to experience His love in a tangible way.

You might also consider incorporating acts of service or compassion into your routine. Volunteering at a local soup kitchen, mentoring a young person, or simply offering a helping hand to a neighbor in need can be powerful expressions of your faith. These acts not only bless others but also deepen your own understanding of God's love and His call to live a life of service and generosity.

Don't also underestimate the power of mentorship in your spiritual growth journey. Finding a trusted guide, someone who has walked the path of faith before you, can be invaluable. A mentor can offer wisdom, encouragement, and accountability, helping you to navigate challenges, to stay focused on your goals, and to deepen your relationship with God.

Seek out someone in your church or community who embodies the qualities you admire and who is willing to invest in your spiritual development. Share your struggles and questions openly, and be receptive to their guidance and feedback. Remember, mentorship is a two-way street. As you learn from your mentor, you also have the opportunity to offer your own unique gifts and perspectives, contributing to their growth as well.

Creating a spiritual growth plan is not a one-size-fits-all endeavor. It's a personal journey that requires self-reflection, intentionality, and a willingness to embrace both the challenges and the rewards of growth. But as you commit to this process, as you seek God's guidance and lean on the support of your community, you will find that your faith deepens, your trust in Him grows stronger, and your ability to navigate life's uncertainties with confidence and hope expands.

Remember, the journey of faith is not about achieving perfection; it's about pursuing a deeper relationship with God, one that is marked by trust, surrender, and a willingness to grow. As you continue on this path, may you find joy in the journey, strength in His presence, and hope in His promises.

Continuously Seeking God's Guidance

Cultivating a listening spirit is essential for those who desire to embrace God's guidance amidst skepticism and uncertainty. It's about tuning our hearts and minds to the frequency of His voice, learning to recognize His whispers amidst the cacophony of the world. It's about creating space in our busy lives for quiet reflection, for intentional listening, and for a deep yearning to know His will.

When we cultivate a listening spirit, we open ourselves to the possibility of divine encounters, those moments when God speaks into the depths of our being, offering wisdom, comfort, and direction. We become more attuned to His presence in our lives, recognizing His fingerprints on the circumstances we face and His gentle nudges towards a path of purpose and fulfillment.

Responding to God's leading is another crucial aspect of embracing His guidance. It's not enough to simply hear His voice; we must also be willing to obey. Obedience, in the context of faith, is not about blind submission or legalistic adherence to rules. It's about a loving response to God's invitation, a willingness to trust His wisdom and to follow His lead, even when it challenges our own understanding or requires us to step outside our comfort zones.

When we obey God's leading, we demonstrate our trust in Him, our belief that He knows what is best for us, even when the path ahead seems unclear. We also open ourselves to the transformative power of His grace, allowing Him to shape us into the people He has created us to be. Obedience, while not always easy, is a pathway to deeper intimacy with God, a way of aligning our hearts and wills with His.

Prayer, as we've explored throughout this book, is a vital tool for seeking and receiving God's guidance. But it's not just about bringing our requests before Him; it's also about cultivating an ongoing dialogue, a continuous conversation with the One who loves us unconditionally and desires to lead us into a life of abundance.

Through prayer, we can express our doubts and uncertainties, our hopes and dreams, and our longing for His presence and guidance. We can ask for wisdom, for clarity, and for the strength to follow His will, even when it challenges our own understanding. We can also listen for His response, trusting that He will speak to us in ways that we can understand, whether through a gentle whisper, a sudden insight, or a deep sense of peace that settles over our hearts.

As you continue on your journey of faith, remember that God is always with you, offering His guidance, His comfort, and His unwavering love. By seeking Him diligently, trusting in His promises, and embracing His leading, you can navigate the uncertainties of life with confidence, knowing that He is the author and perfecter of your faith.

Conclusion

Throughout this transformative exploration of doubt and faith, we've unearthed a profound truth: the journey towards unwavering trust in God is often paved with questions, uncertainties, and even moments of profound struggle. We've discovered that doubt is not the antithesis of faith but a natural companion on the spiritual path, a catalyst for growth, and an invitation to a deeper relationship with our Creator.

From the pages of Scripture, we've encountered biblical figures who wrestled with their own doubts and fears, their stories echoing across the ages and resonating with our own experiences. We've witnessed Abraham's unwavering obedience in the face of the unknown, Jacob's transformative encounter with God, and Job's steadfastness amidst unimaginable suffering. Their journeys, marked by both triumphs and trials, remind us that faith is not a static state but a dynamic process, one that requires courage, perseverance, and a willingness to embrace the uncertainties of life.

We've also explored practical steps for cultivating trust in God, even when doubts linger. We've delved into the power of prayer, the solace of Scripture, the strength of community, and the transformative potential of worship. We've learned to identify the sources of our skepticism, to manage criticism with grace and wisdom, and to fortify our internal convictions through reflection and spiritual practices.

As you close this book, I urge you to continue reflecting on your own journey of faith. Keep a journal of your experiences, documenting the moments of doubt, the glimmers of hope, and the transformative encounters with God that shape your understanding of His love and faithfulness. Write down your prayers, your questions, and your reflections on Scripture, allowing these words to become a tangible record of your spiritual growth.

Remember, faith is not a destination but an ongoing journey. There will be new challenges, unexpected detours, and moments when doubt threatens to overshadow your trust. But in those moments, may you find solace in the truths we've explored together. May you recall the stories of Abraham, Jacob, and Job, and let their journeys remind you of the strength and resilience that can be found in a faith that embraces uncertainty.

As you step into the future, hold onto the hope that comes from trusting in God's plans. Even when the path ahead seems unclear, remember that He is with you, guiding you, and leading you towards a future filled with purpose and fulfillment. Embrace the unknown with courage and conviction, knowing that He is the author and perfecter of your faith.

And so, with hearts filled with hope and minds renewed by His truth, let us continue to walk this journey of faith, embracing God's guidance amidst skepticism and uncertainty, and discovering the boundless possibilities that unfold when we say, **"I Want to Trust, But Just Can't."**